3 YEAR

Classworks
Literacy

Carolyn Bray

Acknowledgements

The author and publishers wish to thank the following for permission to use copyright material:

Bill's New Frock © Anne Fine 1989. Published by Egmont Books Limited, London and used with permission.

The Hodgeheg © Dick King-Smith 1987, reproduced by permission of Penguin Books Limited.

Dimanche Diller. A Small Girl – a Big Adventure © Henrietta Branford, reprinted by permission of HarperCollins Publishers Ltd.

It's Too Frightening For Me! © Shirley Hughes, reproduced by permission of Penguin Books Limited.

Colly's Barn © 1991 Michael Morpurgo. Published by Egmont Books Limited, London and used with permission.

Duncan's Treehouse © Amanda Vassey, reprinted by permission of HarperCollins Publishers Ltd.

'Waves' © Jackie Kay 1992, reproduced by permission of Penguin Books Limited.

'Snake' © Moira Andrew, first published in *My First Oxford Book of Poems*, edited by John Foster, OUP 2000.

Era Publications, Australia, for extracts from Amanda Graham, *Cinderella/Alex & the Glass Slipper*. Copyright © 1991 Amanda Graham.

John Foster for 'The Schoolkids' Rap', from *Word Wizard* by John Foster, Oxford University Press, 2000. Copyright © John Foster 2000.

HarperCollins Publishers for an extract from Henrietta Branford, *Dimanche Diller*, Young Lions 1994.

Anne Hay for Rodney Bennett, 'Windy Nights'.

David Higham Associates on behalf of the Estate of the author for an extract from Roald Dahl, *The Minpins*, Jonathan Cape.

Jack Ousbey for 'Gran Can You Rap?'.

PFD on behalf of the author for Roger McGough, 'The Sound Collector', from *You Tell Me* by Roger McGough. Copyright © Roger McGough 1979.

John Rice for 'Metal Fettle' from *Down at the Dinosaur Fair* by John Rice, Story Chest series, Thomas Nelson 1993.

Cynthia Rider for 'Waterfall', first published in *The Way Through the Woods and Other Poems*, Oxford University Press 2000.

Crown copyright material, 'Internet permission letter' is reproduced under Class Licence C01 W 0000195 with the permission of the Controller of HMSO and the Queen's Printer for Scotland.

Spaghetti Book Club for website book reviews of Roald Dahl's *James and the Giant Peach* and *The BFG*: www.spaghettibookclub.org.

The Random House Group Ltd. for an extract from Shirley Hughes, *Chips and Jessie*, Bodley Head (1985).

Richard James for 'Kitchen Sounds', included in *Sense Poems* ed. John Foster, Oxford University Press (1996).

Frances Lincoln Ltd. for an extract from Eric Madden, *Rainbow Bird* (1993).

The Watts Publishing Group for an extract from Laurence Anholt, *Cinderboy*, Orchard Books (1996).

Cover photo © Royalty-Free/CORBIS.

Contents

Unit	Outcome	Objectives	Page
Poetry Using the Senses	A poem that describes and creates impact	T6, T13	1
Stories with Familiar Settings	A story opening with setting, introducing the characters using dialogue	S3, S5, S7, S8 T1, T2, T10, T11, T12, T16	12
Shape Poems	A shape poem based on fireworks	S3 T6, T7, T8, T14	28
Non-chronological Reports	A class book on aspects of life in Ancient Egypt (linked with QCA History unit 10)	S4, S9, S10, S11, S12 T17, T18, T23	37
Traditional Stories	An alternative version of a traditional story	S2, S3 T1, T2, T3, T7, T9, T10	49
Oral and Performance Poetry	An additional verse for a known poem, to be written and performed	T11	69
Myths	A myth planned and written by ourselves	S2, S3, S6, S7 T1, T6, T9	80
Instruction Texts	A set of instructions for cleaning your teeth	S10, S12, S13 T14, T15, T16	105
Reviewing Books by the Same Author	A book review	S2, S5 T1, T8, T9, T14	118
Letter Writing	A letter (or email) to an author	S3 S7 T16, T20, T21, T23	129
Poetry that Plays with Language	A poem based on a real experience (visit, special event) that uses sound to create effects	T7, T15	152
Adventure Stories	An adventure story in chapters	S4 T1, T2, T10, T11, T13	167

Introduction

How Classworks works

What this book contains

- Chunks of text, both annotated and 'blank' for your own annotations.
- Checklists (or toolkits), planning frames, storyboards, scaffolds and other writing aids.
- Examples of modelled, supported and demonstration writing.
- Lesson ideas including key questions and plenary support.
- Marking ladders for structured self-assessment.
- Blocked unit planning with suggested texts, objectives and outcomes.
- Word-level starter ideas to complement the daily teaching of phonics, handwriting and other skills.
- There are no scripts, no worksheets and nothing you can't change to suit your needs.

How this book is organised

- There are blocked units of work (see previous page) lasting between one week and several, depending on the text type.
- Each blocked unit is organised into a series of chunks of teaching content.
- Each 'chunk' has accompanying checklists and other photocopiable resources.
- For every text we *suggest* annotations, checklists and marking ladders.
- Every unit follows the *teaching sequence for writing* found in *Grammar for Writing* (DfES 2000).
- You can mix and match teaching ideas, units and checklists as you see fit.

How you can use *Classworks* with your medium-term plan

- Refer to your medium-term planning for the blocking of NLS objectives.
- Find the text-type you want to teach (or just the objectives).
- Use the contents page to locate the relevant unit.
- Familiarise yourself with the text and language features using *Classworks* checklists and exemplar analysis pages, and other DfES or QCA resources such as *Grammar for Writing*.
- Browse the lesson ideas and photocopiables to find what you want to use.
- You can just use the text pages … photocopy and adapt the checklists … use or change some of the teaching ideas … take whatever you want and adapt it to fit your class.

Planning a blocked unit of work with Classworks

Classworks units exemplify a blocked unit approach to planning the teaching of Literacy. What follows is an outline of this method of planning and teaching, and how *Classworks* can help you

You need: *Classworks* Literacy Year 3, medium-term planning; OHT (optional).
Optional resources: your own choice of texts for extra analysis; *Grammar for Writing*.

Method

- From the medium-term planning, identify the **outcome**, **texts** and **objectives** you want to teach.

- *Classworks* units **exemplify** how some units could be planned, resourced and taught.

- Decide how to 'chunk' the text you are analysing, for example, introductory paragraph, paragraph 1, paragraph 2, closing paragraph.

- *Classworks* units give an example of **chunking** with accompanying resources and exemplar analysis. Texts for pupil analysis (labelled 'Pupil copymaster') are intended for whole class display on OHT.

- **Whatever you think of the checklists provided, analyse the text with *your* class and build *your own* checklist for the whole text, and for each chunk.**

- Plan your blocked unit based on the following teaching sequence for writing.

- *Classworks* units outline one way of planning a **blocked unit**, with exemplifications of some days, and suggestions for teaching content on others.

Shared Reading – analysing the text – create 'checklist' or writer's toolkit	The children analyse another of that text type and add to checklist	Review checklist
Shared Writing – demonstrate application of 'checklist' to a small piece of writing	The children write independently based on your demonstration	Use examples on OHT to check against the 'checklist'

- This model is only a guideline, allowing the writing process to be scaffolded. You would want to build in opportunities for planning for writing, talking for writing, teaching explicit word-level and sentence-level objectives that would then be modelled in the shared writing, and so on. There are ideas for word-level and sentence-level starters on pages 200–201.

- Allow opportunities for the children to be familiar with the text type. This might include reading plenty of examples, drama, role play, video, and so on.

Assessment

- Make sure that 'checklists' are displayed around the room and referred to before writing and when assessing writing in the **plenary**.

- One or two children could work on an OHT, which could be the focus of the plenary.

- Use a **marking ladder** for the children to evaluate their writing. This is based on the checklist your class has built up. We give you an example of how it might look for each blocked unit. There's a blank copy on page 202.

What each page does

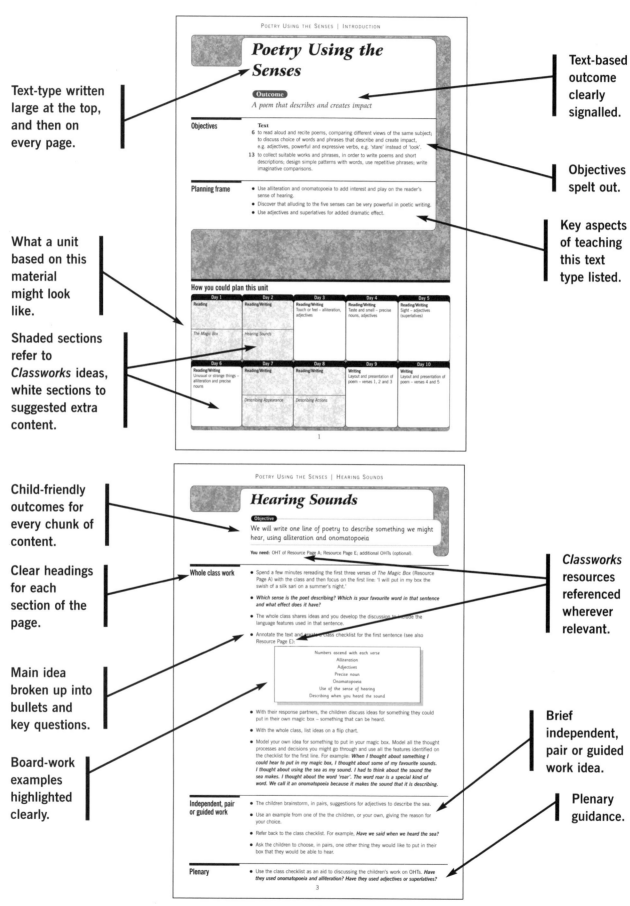

Text-type written large at the top, and then on every page.

Text-based outcome clearly signalled.

Objectives spelt out.

Key aspects of teaching this text type listed.

What a unit based on this material might look like.

Shaded sections refer to *Classworks* ideas, white sections to suggested extra content.

Child-friendly outcomes for every chunk of content.

Clear headings for each section of the page.

Main idea broken up into bullets and key questions.

Board-work examples highlighted clearly.

Classworks resources referenced wherever relevant.

Brief independent, pair or guided work idea.

Plenary guidance.

Poetry Using the Senses

Outcome

A poem that describes and creates impact

Objectives

Text

6 to read aloud and recite poems, comparing different views of the same subject; to discuss choice of words and phrases that describe and create impact, e.g. adjectives, powerful and expressive verbs, e.g. 'stare' instead of 'look'.

13 to collect suitable words and phrases, in order to write poems and short descriptions; design simple patterns with words, use repetitive phrases; write imaginative comparisons.

Planning frame

- Use alliteration and onomatopoeia to add interest and play on the reader's sense of hearing.
- Discover that alluding to the five senses can be very powerful in poetic writing.
- Use adjectives and superlatives for added dramatic effect.

How you could plan this unit

Day 1	Day 2	Day 3	Day 4	Day 5
Reading	Reading/Writing	Reading/Writing Touch or feel – alliteration, adjectives	Reading/Writing Taste and smell – precise nouns, adjectives	Reading/Writing Sight – adjectives (superlatives)
The Magic Box	*Hearing Sounds*			

Day 6	Day 7	Day 8	Day 9	Day 10
Reading/Writing Unusual or strange things – alliteration and precise nouns	Reading/Writing	Reading/Writing	Writing Layout and presentation of poem – verses 1, 2 and 3	Writing Layout and presentation of poem – verses 4 and 5
	Describing Appearance	*Describing Actions*		

The Magic Box

Objective

We will find out what kinds of words a poet chooses when writing poetry about the senses

You need: OHT of Resource Page A; Resource Pages B–E; flip chart or board.

Whole class work	• Show the OHT of *The Magic Box* (Resource Page A) to the class. Read the poem aloud to your class, then read it aloud together.
	• Ask the children to work with response or talking partners to discuss the poem.
	• ***What do you think the poem is about? What is your favourite part and why?***
	• Review the five senses with your class.
	• Return to the OHT of the poem. Read the first three verses aloud together.
	• Ask the the children to identify when the poet describes using senses and annotate the text on the OHT as the children identify the senses (see Resource Page B).
	• When reading the poem aloud, the children could touch their noses if there is a description of a smell, or stick their tongues out when there is a description of taste, and so on.
	• ***Is there anything else you notice about the words the poet has used?***
	• Use questioning to help the children identify some of the language features and annotate on the OHT. This will be the basis for creating your class checklist (see Resource Page E for ideas).
Independent, pair or guided work	• Ask the children to identify the poet's use of senses in *The Magic Box* by annotating the text.
	• Some groups could go on to read *If I had wings* (Resource Page C) and identify independently features that the class has identified together (see Resource Page D).
Plenary	• With the class, recap the list of the five senses that are used in *The Magic Box*.
	• ***Is there anything else we can add to our checklist for writing poetry using our senses – use of simile, powerful verbs and so on?***
	• Review the poem against the checklist that your class has developed.

2

Hearing Sounds

Objective

We will write one line of poetry to describe something we might hear, using alliteration and onomatopoeia

You need: OHT of Resource Page A; Resource Page E; additional OHTs (optional).

Whole class work

- Spend a few minutes rereading the first three verses of *The Magic Box* (Resource Page A) with the class and then focus on the first line: 'I will put in my box the swish of a silk sari on a summer's night.'

- *Which sense is the poet describing? Which is your favourite word in that sentence and what effect does it have?*

- The whole class shares ideas and you develop the discussion to include the language features used in that sentence.

- Annotate the text and create a class checklist for the first sentence (see also Resource Page E):

> Numbers ascend with each verse
> Alliteration
> Adjectives
> Precise noun
> Onomatopoeia
> Use of the sense of hearing
> Describing when you heard the sound

- With their response partners, the children discuss ideas for something they could put in their own magic box – something that can be heard.

- With the whole class, list ideas on a flip chart.

- Reread and edit the ideas. Model your own idea for something to put in your magic box. Explain aloud all your thought processes and decisions and use all the features identified on the checklist for the first line. For example:

> I will put in my box the roar of the wild waves on a windy night.

Independent, pair or guided work

- The children brainstorm, in pairs, suggestions for their first sentence.

- Refer back to the class checklist. For example, *Have we said when we heard the sea?*

- Ask the children to choose one thing they would like to put in their box that they would be able to hear. They write a sentence describing this sound using some of the features in the checklist.

Plenary

- Use the class checklist as an aid to discussing the children's work on OHTs. *Have they used onomatopoeia and alliteration? Have they used adjectives or superlatives?*

Describing Appearance

Objective

We will learn to make choices about the words we use to describe what our magic box is made from

You need: Resource Pages A and E; OHTs.

Whole class work

- Spend a few minutes reading verse five of *The Magic Box* (Resource Page A).

- *Shut your eyes – can you imagine the magic box? Has the poet painted a picture with words? What language features (types of words) has the poet used that paint the picture so well? What effect does the use of alliteration have?*

- With your class, annotate the text to identify the language features, and develop your class checklist for poetic usage of words:

> Powerful verbs
>
> Alliteration
>
> Magical and unusual things
>
> Precise nouns

- Model the thought processes for writing your own version of this verse (see example 2, Resource Page E) and then measure it against the checklist.

Independent, pair or guided work

- Ask the children to discuss with response partners some of the materials from which their box could be made.

- The children then work in pairs to write a description of what their box is made from, using the class checklist and your modelled writing as a template for their own writing.

Plenary

- Invite suggestions from the children and write two examples of their work on OHTs. Use the OHT work to measure the the children's choice of language against the class checklist.

Describing Actions

Objective

We will learn to make choices about words and phrases to use to describe what we might do inside our magic box

You need: Resource Pages A and E.

Whole class work

- Spend a few minutes reading the last verse of *The Magic Box* (Resource Page A). Ask the children to discuss it with their response partners.

- *What is it about? What are some of the language features that the poet has used?*

- Make a checklist of language features used (some will have been identified in the previous lesson):

> Powerful verbs
>
> Adjectives
>
> Precise nouns

- Ask the children to discuss with response partners some of the magical things they might do in their magic box. This is an opportunity to discuss the use of powerful verbs.

- Model your own ideas for what you might do in your magic box (see example 3, Resource Page E). As you work, ensure that you:
  - explain all of your thought processes
  - explain your word choices
  - rehearse ideas aloud before writing them
  - reread and edit your work
  - use the language features in the checklist.

Independent, pair or guided work

- Using the class checklist and your modelled writing as a template, ask the children to write their own ideas for the magical things they might do in their magic box.

Plenary

- Use two or three samples of the children's work to assess their writing against the checklist and the modelled example, looking closely at the magical nature of the activities they have chosen.

The Magic Box

I will put in the box

the swish of a silk sari on a summer night,
fire from the nostrils of a Chinese Dragon,
the tip of a tongue touching a tooth.

I will put in the box

a snowman with a rumbling belly,
a sip of the bluest water from Lake Lucerne,
a leaping spark from an electric fish.

I will put in the box

three violet wishes spoken in Gujarati,
the last joke of an ancient uncle
and the first smile of a baby.

I will put in the box

a fifth season and a black sun,
a cowboy on a broomstick
and a witch on a white horse.

My box is fashioned from ice and gold and steel,
with stars on the lid and secrets in the corners.
Its hinges are the toe joints of dinosaurs.

I shall surf in my box
on the great high-rolling breakers of the wild Atlantic,
then wash ashore in a yellow beach
the colour of the sun.

Kit Wright

(Exemplar analysis)

Example of analysis of *The Magic Box*

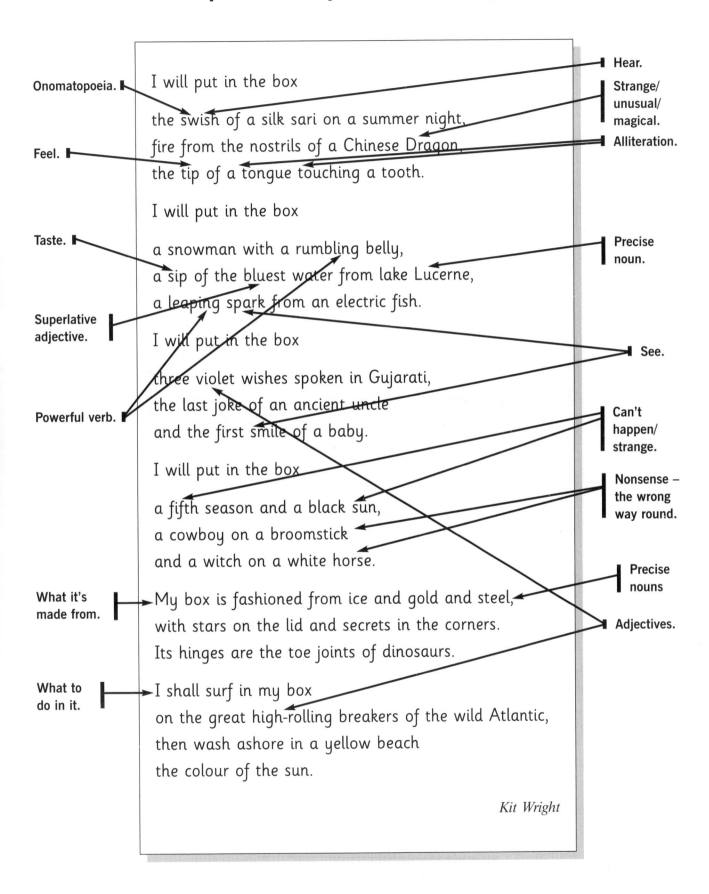

Onomatopoeia.

Feel.

Taste.

Superlative adjective.

Powerful verb.

What it's made from.

What to do in it.

Hear.

Strange/ unusual/ magical.

Alliteration.

Precise noun.

See.

Can't happen/ strange.

Nonsense – the wrong way round.

Precise nouns

Adjectives.

I will put in the box

the swish of a silk sari on a summer night,
fire from the nostrils of a Chinese Dragon,
the tip of a tongue touching a tooth.

I will put in the box

a snowman with a rumbling belly,
a sip of the bluest water from lake Lucerne,
a leaping spark from an electric fish.

I will put in the box

three violet wishes spoken in Gujarati,
the last joke of an ancient uncle
and the first smile of a baby.

I will put in the box

a fifth season and a black sun,
a cowboy on a broomstick
and a witch on a white horse.

My box is fashioned from ice and gold and steel,
with stars on the lid and secrets in the corners.
Its hinges are the toe joints of dinosaurs.

I shall surf in my box
on the great high-rolling breakers of the wild Atlantic,
then wash ashore in a yellow beach
the colour of the sun.

Kit Wright

(Pupil copymaster)

If I Had Wings

If I had wings
I would touch the fingertips of clouds
and glide on the wind.

If I had wings
I would taste a chunk of the sun
as hot as peppered curry.

If I had wings
I would listen to the clouds of a sheep bleat
that graze on the blue.

If I had wings
I would breathe deep and sniff
the scent of raindrops.

If I had wings
I would gaze at the people
who cling to the earth.

If I had wings
I would dream of
walking the deserts
and swimming the seas.

Pie Corbett

(Exemplar analysis)

Example of analysis of *If I Had Wings*

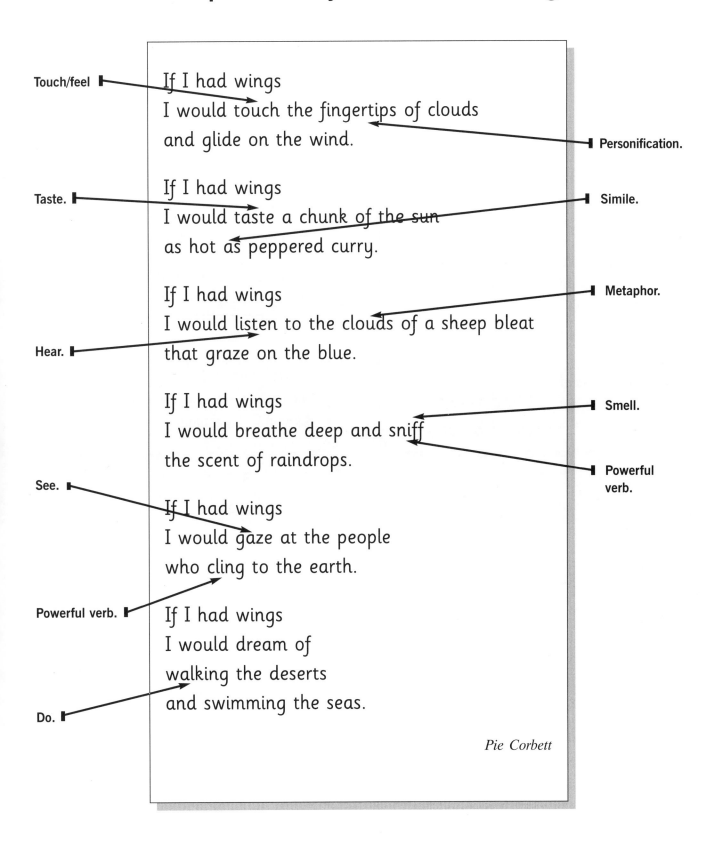

Touch/feel

If I had wings
I would touch the fingertips of clouds
and glide on the wind.

Personification.

Taste.

If I had wings
I would taste a chunk of the sun
as hot as peppered curry.

Simile.

Metaphor.

If I had wings
I would listen to the clouds of a sheep bleat
that graze on the blue.

Hear.

Smell.

If I had wings
I would breathe deep and sniff
the scent of raindrops.

Powerful verb.

See.

If I had wings
I would gaze at the people
who cling to the earth.

Powerful verb.

If I had wings
I would dream of
walking the deserts
and swimming the seas.

Do.

Pie Corbett

Classworks Literacy Year 3 © Carolyn Bray, Nelson Thornes Ltd 2003

(Exemplar material)

Checklist and models for poetry using the senses

 Example of a checklist for writing a poem about the senses ①

Describe something you can:

- hear
- see
- smell
- taste
- touch or feel

Use:

- alliteration
- onomatopoeia
- adjectives
- precise nouns
- powerful verbs

Example of modelling a verse describing appearance ②

My box is crafted from glass and granite and gold,
With rubies on the lid and rainbows in the corners.
Its hinges are the jawbones of cobras.

Example of modelling a verse describing actions ③

I shall sail in my box
Over the raging, mountainous waves of the stormy Pacific,
Then anchor off a tropical island
Surrounded by a turquoise sea.

(**Marking ladder**)

Name: _____

Pupil	Objective	Teacher
	My magic box poem describes something I can: • hear • see • smell • taste • touch or feel.	
	I used: • alliteration • onomatopoeia • adjectives • precise nouns • powerful verbs.	
	My box contains some things that are strange or magical.	
	I described what it is made from.	
	I described what I might do in my box.	
	I discussed my choice of words with my partner.	
	My poem is set out as it should be with the correct punctuation.	
	What could I do to improve my poem next time?	

Classworks Literacy Year 3 © Carolyn Bray, Nelson Thornes Ltd 2003

Stories with Familiar Settings

Outcome

A story opening with setting, introducing the characters using dialogue

Objectives

Sentence

3 [be taught] the function of verbs in sentences through: noticing that sentences cannot make sense without them; collecting and classifying examples of verbs from reading and own knowledge; experimenting with changing simple verbs in sentences and discussing their impact on meaning.

5 to use the term 'verb' appropriately.

7 [be taught] the basic conventions of speech punctuation through: identifying speech marks in reading; beginning to use in own writing; using capital letters to mark the start of direct speech.

8 to use the term 'speech marks'.

Text

1 to compare a range of story settings and to select words and phrases that describe scenes.

2 [be taught] how dialogue is presented in stories, e.g. through statements, questions, exclamations.

10 using reading as a model, to write own passages of dialogue.

11 to develop the use of settings in own stories by: writing short descriptions of known places; writing a description in the style of a familiar story.

12 to investigate and collect sentences/phrases for story openings and endings – use some of these formal elements in retelling and story writing.

16 to begin to organise stories into paragraphs; to begin to use paragraphing in presentation of dialogue in stories.

Planning frame

- Analyse story settings, identifying and using their component parts.
- Write story settings using checklist.

How you could plan this unit

Day 1	Day 2	Day 3	Day 4	Day 5
Reading Collecting and sorting story openings into setting, character or action	**Sentence level – verbs** e.g. *Grammar for Writing*, Unit 1	**Reading and analysing**	**Writing**	**Reading and analysing**
		Dimanche Diller	*The Weather*	*Spotting the Senses*

Day 6	Day 7	Day 8	Day 9	Day 10
Writing	**Reading and analysing** Dialogue for characters	**Sentence level – speech punctuation** e.g. *Grammar for Writing*, Unit 4	**Writing** Dialogue for characters – focus on what they are saying	**Writing** Dialogue for characters – focus on what the character is doing as they are speaking
Using the Senses				

Dimanche Diller

Objective

We will investigate what kinds of words authors use to describe the setting in a story

You need: Resource Pages A–D and I; flip chart.

Whole class work

- Read the opening of *Dimanche Diller* (Resource Page A) and discuss what we know about the setting from this description.

- *What time of year is it? How do we know?*
  What time of day is it? How do we know?
  What's the weather like? How do we know?

- Use the children's responses and location of words and phrases in the text to begin to annotate the text (see Resource Page B) and to start building a class checklist of features (see Resource Page I for ideas).

- Develop the checklist by asking the children to discuss in pairs any words they can find that help to describe the setting for the reader. (The use of powerful verbs is covered in the previous lesson.)

- You may want to spend a little time explaining onomatopoeia if the children need reminding.

- It is unlikely that a child will know the correct term 'simile' and you might take the opportunity to introduce it and add it to the checklist. Although simile might seem quite a difficult language concept, many children hear it being used in everyday spoken language. Refer to some common similes, for example, as weak as water, as cold as ice, as thin as a rake, and so on.

Independent, pair or guided work

- The children identify features on the checklist using an additional text, *Colly's Barn* and annotate the text (Resource Pages C and D).

- Always allow the children to refer to your annotated text when working independently.

Plenary

- Return to Resource Page A and review the class checklist. Which language features did the children find that were on the checklist? *Is there anything different to add?*

- The *Colly's Barn* extract does not contain any similes. Ask the children, in pairs, to think of a simile for the first sentence:

> All night, as the storm raged outside like a _____, the birds in the barn huddled together in their nests.

The Weather

Objective

We will write a story setting that describes the weather

You need: Resource Page I; OHTs (optional).

Whole class work

- Ask the children, in pairs, to recall two features that were on the checklist from the previous lesson. Measure against checklist 1 (Resource Page I) and sort out any misconceptions, for example, the children not understanding the terminology: 'onomatopoeia', 'adjective', and so on.

- Model the writing of a planning grid and a setting (examples 2 and 3, Resource Page I), explaining all of the decisions you make as a writer, including:
  - giving the children the 'big picture': ***What do you want your writing to do when it is finished?*** For example, "I want to describe a beach on a sunny day"
  - thinking the sentence through in your head and saying it to someone before writing
  - reading back your sentence to check it makes sense and is as good as you can make it
  - going through each of the word choices, for example, which verb, adjective to use and why
  - demonstrating spelling strategies for tricky words
  - making deliberate mistakes to reinforce learning
  - demonstrating letter formation and joining when appropriate
  - always referring the children back to the checklist.

- Working with their response partners, the children briefly discuss the modelled writing and suggest alternative powerful verbs or similes at the appropriate stage.

- Prepare the children for their own writing by completing the planning grid (example 4, Resource Page I) and discussing appropriate powerful verbs, onomatopoeia, and so on, before their independent writing. (It is easier to use the same setting, that is, the beach, and just change the time of year, time of day and weather.)

Independent, pair or guided work

- The children work together to discuss and write their opening line on whiteboards, and then feedback briefly before working independently.

- Using the planning grid, the modelled writing and the checklist as a support, ask the children to write a setting based on the planning grid. Some groups could write directly onto an OHT.

Plenary

- Use the writing on the OHT to measure against the checklist. Focus on the use of powerful verbs to reinforce work from the previous lessons.

- Ask other children to read out their opening sentences. The children save their work for use in a later lesson.

Spotting the Senses

Objective

We will find out how authors use their senses to describe settings

You need: Resource Pages A, C and E–H.

Whole class work

- Review the five senses with your class.

- Read together the excerpt from *The Hodgeheg* (Resource Page E). Read again and ask the children to spot when the author writes about the senses. When 'smell' is mentioned, the children put their hands on their noses; for touch, they put their hands together, and so on.

- Ask the children to talk to their response partner about what they think Max saw, heard, smelt, tasted, touched or felt in his little adventure. Use of senses can be added to the class checklist from Day 4.

- When taking responses, ensure that the children use evidence from the text to back up their answers.

- Ask the children if they can find anything else in the text that is also on the class checklist, for example, ensure that they are aware that powerful verbs, adjectives, alliteration, simile and onomatopoeia are still used. Refer to Resource Page F.

- In pairs, the children return to the excerpts from *Dimanche Diller* and *Colly's Barn* (Resource Pages A and C). Ask the children to find out how the author uses the senses to describe these settings.

Independent, pair or guided work

- Using *Duncan's Treehouse* (Resource Page G), ask the children to identify features of the checklist within the extract and annotate the text. Refer to Resource Page H.

Plenary

- Allow the children to give examples of items for the checklist they have found in the text. You can make this exercise into a game to help kinaesthetic learners. For example: *Go to the red corner if you have a good example of some alliteration, the blue corner if you have found a good example of describing what could be smelt in that setting.*

- Is there anything else the children can add to the 'settings' checklist?

Using the Senses

Objective

We will learn how to write a setting using the senses to describe it

You need: Resource Page I; whiteboards and pens for the children, or notebooks; flip chart; children's opening sentences from previous lesson.

Whole class work

- Review the class checklist. How many features can the children remember?

- Read the shared writing from earlier in the unit (see example 3, Resource Page I) and review the use of language features that focused on time of day and weather.

- *Now shut your eyes as I read it again. Imagine being there. What else can you see, taste, smell, touch or hear?* Ask the children to discuss this with their response partner. Take some feedback, focusing each time on a specific sense.

- Model the next part of the setting that focuses on describing using the senses, and introduces the names of the characters (see example 5, Resource Page I).

- As you model the writing make sure that you:
  - explain you had imagined being there at the beach and thought about what you might hear, see and smell, before you did any writing
  - demonstrate jotting down ideas and notes before turning them into sentences
  - rehearse the sentences before writing – speak them aloud, and check for sense
  - demonstrate drafting your ideas and then improving them by experimenting with using powerful verbs, adjectives, alliteration, similes and onomatopoeia
  - explain your reasons for particular word choices
  - reread your work to ensure that ideas are linked and that punctuation is correct
  - demonstrate re-ordering a sentence
  - explain which senses you are using to describe the setting.

Independent, pair or guided work

- With response partners, the children brainstorm ideas about what they might see, hear, smell, taste or touch at the setting for which they wrote an opening sentence.

- You may want to note ideas on a flip chart when taking feedback, to aid those who will struggle with ideas when working independently.

- Use one idea and, with their response partner, ask the children to construct orally a sentence using a powerful verb/adjective/alliteration, depending on ability. Demonstrate this first. For example, "I could hear the leaves on the ground" might be: "The dry, brown sycamore leaves crackled and crunched as children ran through them."

- Independently, the children create the next part of the setting, focusing on using the senses. Remind them to read their opening sentences to make sure their work follows on and to include the names of two children. It is helpful to have one boy and one girl character, as this can lead to more variation in characterisation.

- Have an ice-cream tub of names for the children to choose from for occasions like this as they can spend the whole session deciding which best friend to include!

Plenary

- The children read a phrase or sentence from their work and the rest of the class indicate which sense they are using by pointing to ears, eyes, nose, fingers or mouth.

- Discuss what language features have been used and why they are effective.

(**Pupil copymaster**)

Dimanche Diller

In a matter of seconds the sea had turned from blue to purple, and billows of black clouds had blotted out the summer sky ... At that very moment a monster of a wave, as strong as steel, rose high above the little boat, hung for a moment like a cliff of glass, and crashed onto the deck. It cracked the boat from stem to stern, splintered the mast, ripped through the sails, and tore baby Dimanche from her mother's arms, casting the lifeboat and its precious cargo adrift upon the sea.

... All night the great waves surged, tossing the lifeboat like a cork. Salt sea spray soaked Dimanche's blanket, and an east wind turned her tiny face and hands to ice.

from Dimanche Diller. A Small Girl – A Big Adventure, *by Henrietta Branford*

(Exemplar analysis)

Example of analysis of *Dimanche Diller*

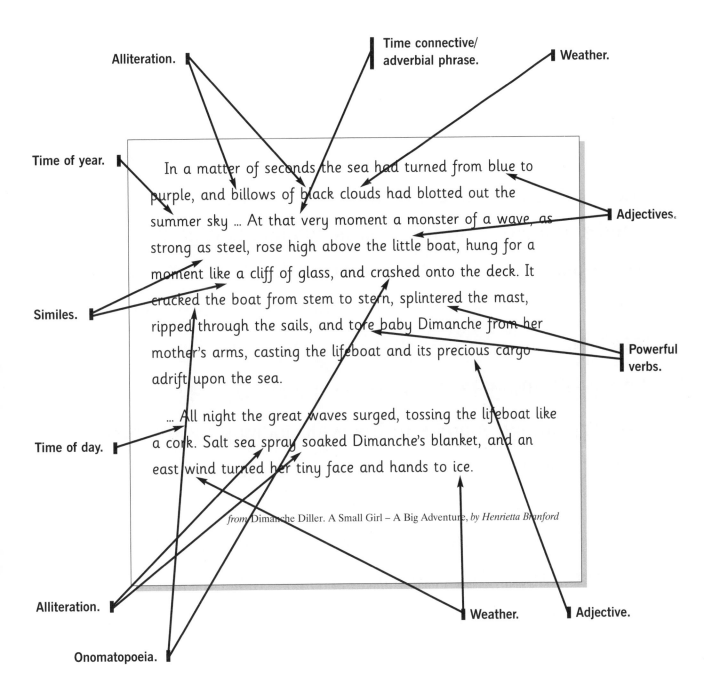

Alliteration.

Time connective/ adverbial phrase.

Weather.

Time of year.

In a matter of seconds the sea had turned from blue to purple, and billows of black clouds had blotted out the summer sky ... At that very moment a monster of a wave, as strong as steel, rose high above the little boat, hung for a moment like a cliff of glass, and crashed onto the deck. It cracked the boat from stem to stern, splintered the mast, ripped through the sails, and tore baby Dimanche from her mother's arms, casting the lifeboat and its precious cargo adrift upon the sea.

... All night the great waves surged, tossing the lifeboat like a cork. Salt sea spray soaked Dimanche's blanket, and an east wind turned her tiny face and hands to ice.

from Dimanche Diller. A Small Girl – A Big Adventure, *by Henrietta Branford*

Adjectives.

Similes.

Powerful verbs.

Time of day.

Alliteration.

Weather.

Adjective.

Onomatopoeia.

(**Pupil copymaster**)

Colly's Barn

All night, as the storm raged outside, the birds in the barn huddled together in their nests, burying their heads in each other to blot out the sound of the thunder. The wind whined and whistled through the eaves, the walls shuddered and the beams creaked and groaned. But Screecher and Colly were not worried. They'd been through storms like this before and the old barn had held together.

Screecher thought the worst of it was over. He was peering through a crack in the wall, looking for the first light of dawn on the distant hills, when the lightning struck. In one blinding flash night was turned to day. A deafening clap of thunder shook the barn and a fireball glowing orange and blue rolled around the barn and disappeared through the door.

from Colly's Barn, *by Michael Morpurgo*

(Exemplar analysis)

Example of analysis of *Colly's Barn*

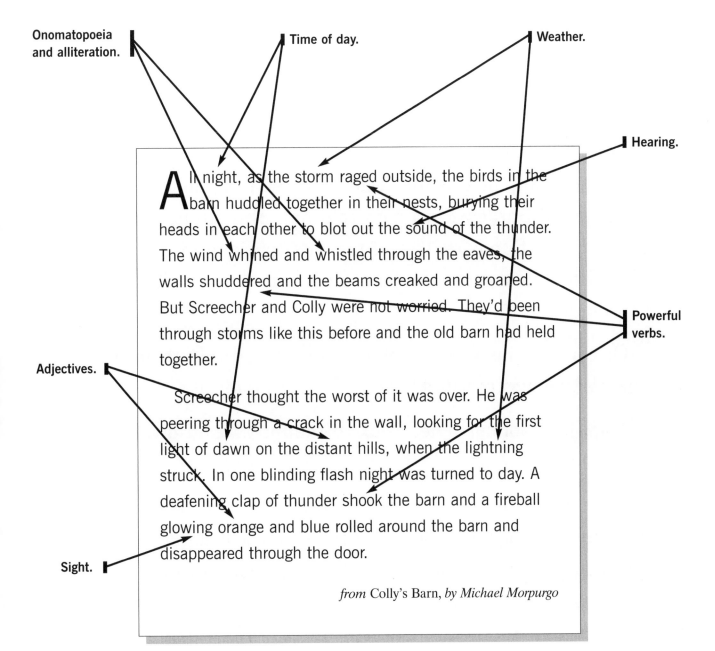

Onomatopoeia and alliteration.

Time of day.

Weather.

Hearing.

Powerful verbs.

Adjectives.

Sight.

All night, as the storm raged outside, the birds in the barn huddled together in their nests, burying their heads in each other to blot out the sound of the thunder. The wind whined and whistled through the eaves, the walls shuddered and the beams creaked and groaned. But Screecher and Colly were not worried. They'd been through storms like this before and the old barn had held together.

Screecher thought the worst of it was over. He was peering through a crack in the wall, looking for the first light of dawn on the distant hills, when the lightning struck. In one blinding flash night was turned to day. A deafening clap of thunder shook the barn and a fireball glowing orange and blue rolled around the barn and disappeared through the door.

from Colly's Barn, *by Michael Morpurgo*

(**Pupil copymaster**)

The Hodgeheg

In the light of a full moon he could see before him a wide stretch of grass and he ran across it until the noise and the stink of the traffic were left behind …

His nose told him of the scent of flowers (in the Ornamental Gardens), his eyes told him of a strange-shaped building (the Bandstand), and his ears told him of the sound of splashing water (as the fountain spouted endlessly in the Lily Pond).

Of course! This was the place that Pa had told them all about! This was the Park!

"Hip, hip roohay!" cried Max to the moon, and away he ran.

For the next few hours he trotted busily about the Park, shoving his snout into everything. Like most children, he was not only nosy but noisy too, and at the sound of his coming the mice scuttled under the Bandstand, the snakes slid away through the Ornamental Gardens and the frogs plopped in to the safe depths of the Lily Pond. Max caught nothing.

from The Hodgeheg, *by Dick King Smith*

(Exemplar analysis)

Example of analysis of *The Hodgeheg*

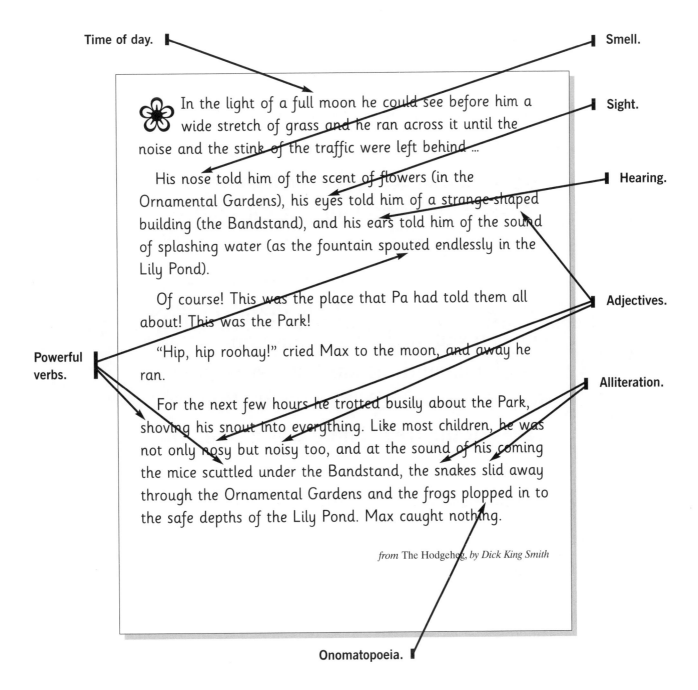

Time of day.

Smell.

Sight.

Hearing.

Adjectives.

Powerful verbs.

Alliteration.

In the light of a full moon he could see before him a wide stretch of grass and he ran across it until the noise and the stink of the traffic were left behind ...

His nose told him of the scent of flowers (in the Ornamental Gardens), his eyes told him of a strange-shaped building (the Bandstand), and his ears told him of the sound of splashing water (as the fountain spouted endlessly in the Lily Pond).

Of course! This was the place that Pa had told them all about! This was the Park!

"Hip, hip roohay!" cried Max to the moon, and away he ran.

For the next few hours he trotted busily about the Park, shoving his snout into everything. Like most children, he was not only nosy but noisy too, and at the sound of his coming the mice scuttled under the Bandstand, the snakes slid away through the Ornamental Gardens and the frogs plopped in to the safe depths of the Lily Pond. Max caught nothing.

from The Hodgeheg, *by Dick King Smith*

Onomatopoeia.

(Pupil copymaster)

Duncan's Treehouse

When Duncan woke, the sun was streaming through the window. The birds in the tree were singing and bickering and calling to each other.

"Wake up!" said Duncan, "it's a beautiful morning."

Duncan and Buster sat outside the front door and shared the midnight feast. Duncan watched a fisherman on the river bank, and the swallows swooping over the water. A breeze rustled the leaves of the tree. There was a smell of damp earth, and everything looked sparkling after the rain.

from Duncan's Treehouse, *by Amanda Vessey*

(Exemplar analysis)

Example of analysis of *Duncan's Treehouse*

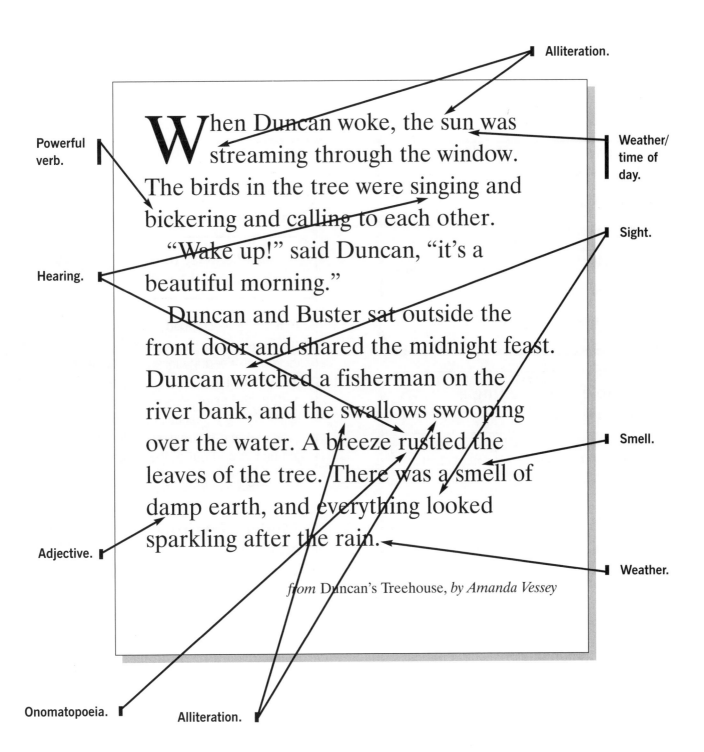

Alliteration.

Powerful verb.

Weather/ time of day.

When Duncan woke, the sun was streaming through the window. The birds in the tree were singing and bickering and calling to each other.
   "Wake up!" said Duncan, "it's a beautiful morning."
   Duncan and Buster sat outside the front door and shared the midnight feast. Duncan watched a fisherman on the river bank, and the swallows swooping over the water. A breeze rustled the leaves of the tree. There was a smell of damp earth, and everything looked sparkling after the rain.

from Duncan's Treehouse, by Amanda Vessey

Hearing.

Sight.

Smell.

Adjective.

Weather.

Onomatopoeia.

Alliteration.

(Exemplar material)

Checklist and models for stories with familiar settings

Example of a checklist for writing a setting

- Tell the time of day or year
- Tell the weather
- Use senses: hear, see, smell, taste, touch or feel
- Use alliteration
- Use powerful verbs
- Use adjectives
- Use onomatopoeia
- Use simile

Example of modelling a planning grid ②

Where is the setting?	The beach
What time of year is it?	August
What time of day is it?	Afternoon
What is the weather like?	Hot, sunny

Modelled writing of a setting (based on grid above) ③

It was a hot, cloudless afternoon. The August sunshine beamed on to brightly coloured beach towels scattered on the sand. Hungry seagulls screeched and swooped over the sea. On the shoreline, children peered into rock-pools and jumped the waves like ponies.

Example of modelling a planning grid

Where is the setting?	The beach
What is the time of year?	Winter
What is the time of day?	Night
What is the weather like?	Stormy

Modelled writing of a setting (based on grid above) ⑤

Tom and Ellie stepped gingerly over the smelly, slimy seaweed towards the rockpools. Peering closely into a clear pool, they saw crabs scuttling, shrimps darting and anemones wobbling like jellies. Hungry seagulls screeched overhead and toddlers squealed as they jumped in and out of the breaking waves.

Modelled writing of dialogue ⑥

"Look what I've found!" yelled Tom excitedly. He reached for his net and started peering into the pool again.

"Rockpools are boring, let's go swimming," called Ellie. She threw down her net and clambered over the rock to the sea.

(**Marking ladder**)

Name: _____

Pupil	Objective	Teacher
	My story opening includes a setting using the time of day and/or time of year.	
	I described what the weather is like.	
	I described what you can see, hear, smell, touch, taste.	
	I used powerful verbs.	
	I used adjectives.	
	I used similes.	
	I used alliteration.	
	I used onomatopoeia.	
	My story opening includes two named characters.	
	I used dialogue, with correct punctuation.	
	I used a powerful verb following the speech.	
	I said what they are doing (when they are speaking) using powerful verbs.	
	What could I do to improve my story opening next time?	

Shape Poems

Outcome

A shape poem based on fireworks

Objectives

Sentence

3 [be taught] the function of verbs in sentences through collecting and classifying examples of verbs from reading and own knowledge, e.g. 'run', 'chase', 'sprint'; 'eat', 'consume', 'gobble'; 'said', 'whispered', 'shrieked'.

Text

6 to read aloud and recite poems, comparing different views of the same subject; to discuss choice of words and phrases that describe and create impact, e.g. adjectives, powerful and expressive verbs, e.g. 'stare' instead of 'look'.

7 to distinguish between rhyming and non-rhyming poetry and comment on the impact of layout.

8 to express their views about a story or poem identifying specific words and phrases to support their viewpoint.

14 to invent calligrams and a range of shape poems, selecting appropriate words and careful presentation. Build up class collections.

Planning frame

- Identify sorts of words used in a shape poem.

- Choose words and phrases to describe a firework.

- Combine ideas and phrases to complete a poem.

Note

- This unit will be most effective if taught following Bonfire Night or another celebration where the children will have seen fireworks. If the children are not able to experience fireworks, then the shared writing example will need to reflect another experience that the children can draw on.

How you could plan this unit

Day 1	Day 2	Day 3	Day 4	Day 5
Reading	**Talk for writing** Brainstorm words and phrases for fireworks. What can you see? What can you hear?	Writing	**Writing** Turning ideas into phrases for the poem using checklist features (Resource Page E). Focus on what the firework sounds like – use of onomatopoeia	**Writing** Presentation of poem. Making phrases and ideas fit the 'shape'
Waves		*Fireworks*		

Waves

Objectives

We will investigate shape poems. We will also investigate the types of words a poet uses in a shape poem so we can write our own

You need: Resources Pages A–E; OHT and whiteboards.

Whole class work

- Present the children with the shape poem *Waves* (Resource Page A).

- *Why do you think it is called a 'shape poem'?* Establish that the words are written in the shape of the subject of the poem. Discuss the difference between a shape poem and a calligram (see example 3, Resource Page E).

- Read the poem together. *Do you like it? Why? Why not?*

- Read the poem together again and ask the children to think about which is their favourite word or phrase in the poem and why.

- With response partners, the children discuss their favourite word or phrase, explaining why. Take feedback from a few pairs.

- Ask the children to discuss with response partners any special types of words they can find that the poet has used. You may need to prompt the children by asking:
  - *What words has the poet used to describe the waves?*
  - *What sounds do the waves make?*
  - *Does the poem rhyme?*

- Discuss other words the poet could have used (synonyms) to check understanding and develop vocabulary.

- Ensure that children with special needs have a copy of the poem in front of them, rather than having to look at the OHT. This will help them to focus on the text.

- Begin building a class checklist of the language features in the poem (see Resource Pages B and E for ideas).

Independent, pair or guided work

- The children read *Snake* (Resource Page C) to identify language features in the checklist. The children highlight the features and annotate the text just as you discussed in the whole class work. Give one pair an OHT of the poem to highlight and annotate.

- *Which checklist features did they find that matched the class checklist? Which were the same? Were there any different ones?* Refer to Resource Page D.

Plenary

- Hide the class checklist. Give the children, working with response partners, one minute to come up with as many checklist features as they can. (These could be written on whiteboards.)

- Ask the children to find examples of the language features in the checklist from their independent work and the whole class work to add to the class checklist: powerful verbs, for example 'coils', 'pounds'; adjectives, for example, 'forked', 'calm', and so on.

Fireworks

Objective

We will use carefully chosen words and phrases to describe what a firework looks like, to include in our own shape poem.

You need: Resource Page E; flip chart; pictures and posters of fireworks; OHTs.

Whole class work

- Review some of the ideas collected from the brainstorm in the previous lesson.

- With response partners, the children revise three features in your class checklist. *Which of the words in our brainstorm are adjectives, powerful verbs, onomatopoeia, and so on?* Ask the children to come up and highlight appropriate words on the flip chart.

- Explain that the class checklist and the children's ideas will be used to develop carefully chosen phrases for a shape poem. *We're not going to worry about putting them into the shape until we have some really good phrases that use what the checklist says we need.*

- Ask the children to identify any words in the brainstorm that might describe what a Catherine wheel looks like.

- Using example 2, Resource Page E, model how to turn ideas from the brainstorm into carefully chosen phrases to describe what the Catherine wheel looks like, using the features from the checklist.

- During the modelled writing:
  - refer back to the brainstorm of ideas from the previous lesson
  - continually refer to the class checklist and ask the children which language feature you have just used
  - explain aloud each of your word choices
  - read and reread work
  - demonstrate the drafting process
  - try out phrases orally before putting them to paper
  - use the opportunity to review relevant spelling patterns or rules, for example, doubling final consonant before adding 'ing'.

Independent, pair or guided work

- The children work with a response partner to decide which firework they want to write about, and write two or three words from the brainstorm, or their own ideas, on to a whiteboard.

- The children work with a response partner to turn ideas and words into two or three phrases that describe what the firework looks like, using the class checklist.

- Two pairs write on to an OHT.

Plenary

- All children check their work against the checklist and tick the features they have used. Ask some children for examples of these features.

- Use the work done on the OHTs to reinforce the checklist, for example, *Who can find me some alliteration in this work?* If the work on the OHT does not use all the checklist features, use this opportunity to demonstrate the drafting process and for the class to help the poets to improve their work.

(**Pupil copymaster**)

Waves

There are waves to chase and waves that crash,

There are waves to jump like skipping ropes,

Waves to run away to sand, waves to leap and bound,

Waves that are turquoise, waves that are brown,

Waves full of seaweed, waves that drown.

Waves clear and calm, waves angry and wronged,

Waves that whisper, waves that roar like thunder

Waves you'd never swim under, pounding rock and shore

Waves that put you to sleep, sssh sssh sssh cradle-rock.

Waves that look like sea horses or sheep or curly froth.

Waves that are cold as bare floor, waves that are warm as toast.

There are waves called the Black Sea, the Red Sea, the North Sea,

Waves called the Pacific Ocean, the Atlantic Ocean, the Antarctic.

If you counted them all, wave upon wave upon wave

Would it be a hundred, a thousand, a billion – or more?

Jackie Kay

(Exemplar analysis)

Example of analysis of *Waves*

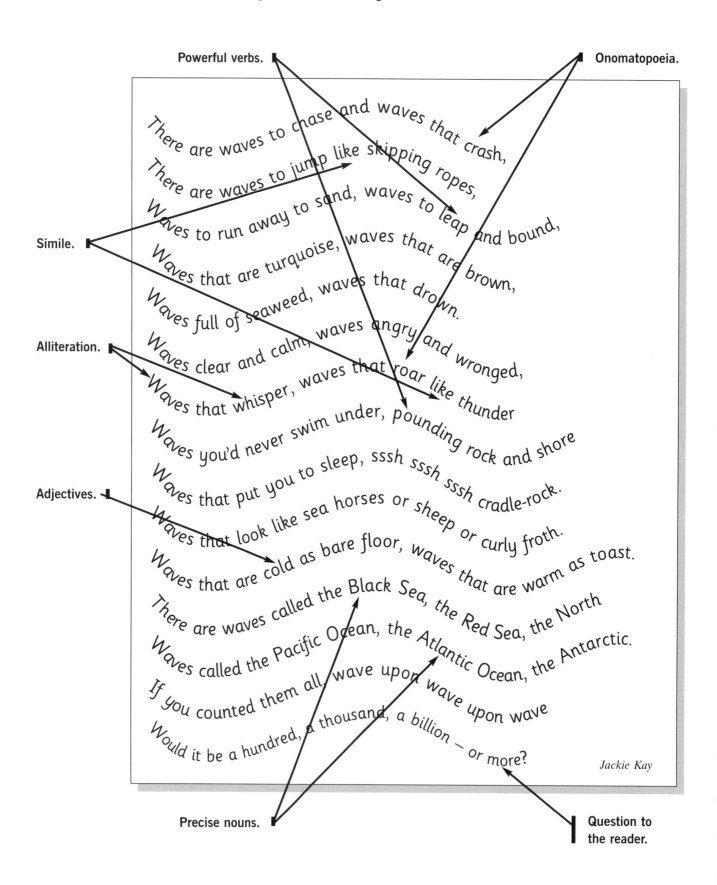

Powerful verbs.

Onomatopoeia.

Simile.

Alliteration.

Adjectives.

There are waves to chase and waves that crash,
There are waves to jump like skipping ropes,
Waves to run away to sand, waves to leap and bound,
Waves that are turquoise, waves that are brown,
Waves full of seaweed, waves that drown.
Waves clear and calm, waves angry and wronged,
Waves that whisper, waves that roar like thunder
Waves you'd never swim under, pounding rock and shore
Waves that put you to sleep, sssh sssh sssh cradle-rock.
Waves that look like sea horses or sheep or curly froth.
Waves that are cold as bare floor, waves that are warm as toast.
There are waves called the Black Sea, the Red Sea, the North
Waves called the Pacific Ocean, the Atlantic Ocean, the Antarctic.
If you counted them all, wave upon wave upon wave
Would it be a hundred, a thousand, a billion – or more?

Jackie Kay

Precise nouns.

Question to the reader.

Snake

Snake slithers
    among stones,
        coils and loops
           and hisses
        forked tongue
    darts as fast
as an arrow,
    aims and misses.

Snake glides
    over pebbles,
        sleeps, snoozing
           in the sun,
        hunger long-
    forgotten
waits still, till
    day is done.

Moira Andrew

(Exemplar analysis)

Example of analysis of *Snake*

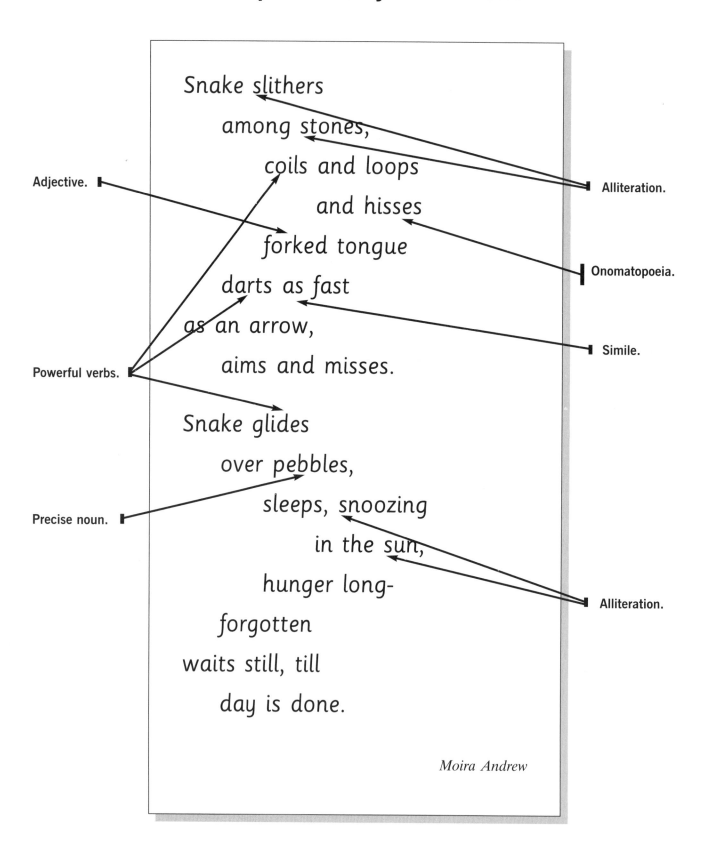

Snake slithers
among stones,
coils and loops
and hisses
forked tongue
darts as fast
as an arrow,
aims and misses.
Snake glides
over pebbles,
sleeps, snoozing
in the sun,
hunger long-
forgotten
waits still, till
day is done.

Moira Andrew

Adjective.

Alliteration.

Onomatopoeia.

Simile.

Powerful verbs.

Precise noun.

Alliteration.

(Exemplar material)

Checklist and models for shape poems

Example of a checklist for a shape poem

- Use adjectives
- Use powerful verbs
- Use onomatopoeia
- Use simile
- Use alliteration
- Use precise nouns
- Use some rhyming
- Write the poem in the shape of the subject

Example of modelling a shape poem

An orange and yellow lollipop
A wild, whizzing wheel
Spinning faster and faster
Sparks falling like silver raindrops

Example of a calligram

Shape poems are written in the shape of the subject, whereas calligrams are words that have been written in a certain way so that their meaning is echoed in the design, for example, shiver.

(**Marking ladder**)

Name: _____

Pupil	Objective	Teacher
	My shape poem uses well-chosen words.	
	I used powerful verbs.	
	I used adjectives.	
	I used alliteration.	
	I used onomatopoeia.	
	I used simile.	
	I used precise nouns.	
	I used some rhyming words.	
	I used a layout that is the shape of the subject.	
	What could I do to improve my poem next time?	

Non-chronological Reports

Outcome

A class book on aspects of life in Ancient Egypt (linked with QCA History unit 10)

Objectives

Sentence

4 to use verb tenses with increasing accuracy in speaking and writing, e.g. 'catch'/'caught', 'see'/'saw', 'go'/'went', etc.

9 to notice and investigate a range of other devices for presenting texts, e.g. speech bubbles, enlarged or italicised print, captions and headings, inset text. Explore purposes and collect examples.

10 to identify the boundaries between separate sentences in reading and their own writing.

11 to write in complete sentences.

12 to demarcate the end of a sentence with a full stop and the start of a new one with a capital letter.

Text

17 to understand the distinction between fact and fiction; to use terms 'fact', 'fiction' and 'non-fiction' appropriately.

18 to notice differences in the style and structure of fiction and non-fiction writing.

23 to write simple non-chronological reports from known information, e.g. from own experience or from texts read, using notes made to organise and present ideas. Write for a known audience, e.g. other pupils in class, teacher, parent.

Planning frame

- Locating factual information from a variety of sources.

- Reporting factual information using diagrams, maps, bullet points and so on.

Notes

- This unit needs to be taught alongside the QCA unit on Ancient Egypt as it is content-specific and assumes a level of knowledge.

- It is suggested that children will have worked on the skills of locating information, highlighting key words or phrases in a passage and completing a chart of information gathered, for example, a QUAD grid on an aspect of Egyptian life that they can then use to write their part of the class book.

- This unit is about writing a non-chronological report – organising information in an effective and interesting way to engage the reader. It is too much to ask the children to think about the content of their writing and the organisation *and* use of language features at the same time. Exploiting cross-curricular links with this kind of work is therefore vital.

How you could plan this unit

Day 1	Day 2	Day 3	Day 4	Day 5
Reading	**Writing**	**Reading and writing** Heading for the page. Use of ICT and *Grammar for Writing* Unit 5	**Reading and writing** Introductory paragraph (some children may find it easier to write this at the end of the unit)	**Writing** Consistent use of tense. *Grammar for Writing* Unit 2. (Notes from brainstorm will be in present tense, but report should be in past tense because of historical nature)
Discussing Examples	*Spidergrams*			

Day 6	Day 7	Day 8	Day 9	Day 10
Reading and writing	**Reading and writing**	**Writing** Third paragraph. Subheading as a question. Turning notes into sentences. Use of factual adjectives	**Writing** 'Did you know?' box/ fascinating fact to engage the reader	**Writing** Fourth paragraph. Subheading as a question. Turning notes into sentences. Use of bullet points or commas to list items
Composing Sentences	*Diagrams, Labels and Captions*			

Day 11	Day 12
Writing (optional) Where the children have been working in draft, model revising and editing text	**Writing (optional)** Add contents, glossary and index to class book

Discussing Examples

We will find out how the information in non-chronological reports is organised

You need: Resource Pages A and E; non-fiction texts, for example, *Magic Bean*, *Info Trial*, 'I wonder why' series; IT resources – CD-ROMs, web sites.

Whole class work

- Read together an example of a simple non-chronological report (Resource Page A or one of the sample texts). Briefly review the content, all of which needs to be familiar to the children, so that they can then focus on the language and organisation of the text.

- *We are going to produce a class book about the Ancient Egyptians. To do this we are going to look at examples of how other authors have done it and use their ideas to help us.*

- Use response partners to discuss:
    - *What makes this different from a story book?* Give an example or put a fiction text next to it to help the children identify the differences. This focuses on the organisational aspects of the text.
    - *Why would I want to read this?* This focuses on the purpose of the text.
    - *How does the layout and organisation help the reader to gather information?* This helps the children to understand the link between the purpose of the text and its organisation.

- During the discussion, annotate the text as the children identify the features. This will initiate the writing of your class checklist (see Resource Page E for ideas).

Independent, pair or guided work

- Using a variety of non-fiction texts, the children investigate the features in the checklist and identify any others that could be added to it.

Plenary

- Select one or two features that are proving difficult to identify (for example, labels and captions) and find examples from the children's texts.

- Ask one pair of children to show the rest of the class the features they have found.

- *Is there anything else to add to our checklist?*

Spidergrams

Objective

We will use a spidergram to organise ideas for a page of our Ancient Egypt book

You need: Resource Pages A–C; whiteboards (one per pair); paper; OHTs.

Whole class work

- Use response partners to review briefly the parts of Ancient Egyptian life the children have investigated, for example, food and farming, clothes and fashion, houses, the afterlife, and so on. (The children will have collected information in some form about one or several of these themes.)

- *When you make your page, although you have lots of information, you need to organise it carefully so that a reader can understand it.*

- Use the shared reading text on pyramids, temples and tombs (Resource Page A). *What is this page about? How has the author organised the information? How does the layout help you to understand it?*

- Reinforce the idea that different sections of writing describe one aspect of the subject area.

- Using the spidergram (Resource Page B) and QUAD grid (Resource Page C), model organising information into sections. As you write, ensure that you:
  - explain your thought processes aloud, for example, why you have chosen the categories flooding, boats and river life
  - explain how the categories help you to organise your ideas
  - point out that you are writing in note form. Verbally, put one or two examples of notes into sentences to demonstrate the difference between notes and sentences
  - explain the use of technical words
  - draft and redraft ideas for each category.

- After demonstrating one or two categories, ask the children for suggestions for others.

Independent, pair or guided work

- Before they create their own spidergram, ask the children, in pairs, to choose three categories for their area and record them on a whiteboard in spidergram format. Use 'show me' to assess whether each pair has understood the spidergram.

- Once the spidergram is clearly organised, the children record their own spidergram on paper. One or two pairs work on an OHT.

Plenary

- Use the children's OHTs to evaluate spidergrams. Ask the children to explain the categories they used and their choice of additional categories.

- Take one of their ideas in note form and model writing it as a sentence.

- In pairs, the children verbally practise turning notes into sentences.

Composing Sentences

Objective

We will organise notes into sentences containing information for our non-chronological report

You need: Resource Pages A, B and E; whiteboards (one between two); OHTs.

Whole class work

- Reread the first section of Resource Page A.

- *Why did the Egyptians build pyramids? How many ideas or pieces of information are there in each sentence?*

- Ask individual children to come out and highlight a fact. Discuss that there are only one or two pieces of information or facts in each sentence and that the sentences are quite short and simple.

- Use questioning to build up a class checklist for the first paragraph (see checklist 2, Resource Page E for ideas).

- Refer to the spidergram (Resource Page B). Explain that you are going to turn the notes from the category about flooding into sentences for your report on the Nile.

- Demonstrate turning notes into a sentence verbally, for example: "Nilometer – The Egyptians would measure how high the water in the Nile was rising using a Nilometer."

- Take a word or phrase from the notes, for example, 'black mud'. In pairs, ask the children to rehearse a sentence that uses 'black mud'.

- Demonstrate turning notes into sentences to make a paragraph about flooding (see example 3, Resource Page E). As you write, ensure that you:
  - demonstrate redrafting sentences
  - demonstrate keeping the tense consistent. (One of the best ways of reinforcing this is by making deliberate errors)
  - refer back to the spidergram
  - link the categories on the spidergram with the subheadings
  - reinforce using full stops and capital letters. Again, include deliberate errors.

- The children refer to the class checklist to identify the features you have used.

Independent, pair or guided work

- In pairs, the children choose one of the notes from their spidergram and orally turn it into a sentence. They write the sentence on a whiteboard.

- In pairs, the children compose sentences from their notes on their whiteboards and decide a subheading for the paragraph. Record the work either by photocopying or by the children rewriting on to paper. One or two pairs can write on an OHT.

- Check that the methodology has been understood before allowing the children to work independently.

Plenary

- Give the children one minute to write as many features from the checklist for paragraphs on their whiteboards.

- Use the sample work from the OHTs to check use of subheading and sentences.

- The children tick the features they have used from the checklist on their own work.

Diagrams, Labels and Captions

Objective

We will learn how to use pictures, diagrams, labels and captions to help the reader gather information from our book

You need: Resource Pages A, D and E; non-fiction texts, for example, *Magic Bean*, *Info Trial*, 'I wonder why' series.

Whole class work

- Refer to Resource Page A and the non-fiction books discussed earlier.

- *Why do we use diagrams and pictures in non-fiction texts?* Clarify the difference between pictures and diagrams.

- *What is the job of labels and captions?* Clarify the difference between a label and a caption.

- Discuss presentational devices for diagrams, for example, print for the labels, leader lines drawn with a ruler and horizontal wherever possible, clear and simple diagrams.

- Begin to develop a class checklist (see checklist 4, Resource Page E for ideas).

- Using the diagram of a Nilometer (Resource Page D), demonstrate the use of the features identified in the checklist.

- Draw a diagram of a Nilometer and add labels ('river bank', 'stone steps', 'River Nile', 'land') and a caption:

> Along the banks of the River Nile were stone steps which measured the depth of the River Nile. They were called Nilometers.

- During shared writing, ensure that you:
  - explain aloud all your thought processes, for example, why you have chosen to draw a diagram of the Nilometer
  - explain which words you want to use as the labels – are they key words? Add red herrings to check that the children understand the meaning and purpose of key words
  - demonstrate the wrong way (and right way) of drawing leader lines
  - orally rehearse the caption before writing.

Independent, pair or guided work

- In pairs, the children discuss what diagram might be useful for their page, and how it will help the reader. Take feedback.

- The children decide who is going to draw and label the diagram, and who is going to work on the caption.

Plenary

- In pairs, the children swap with others to see if they have used everything on the class checklist. *Can you tell what the subject of the page might be from the diagram and captions?*

Pupil copymaster

PYRAMIDS, TEMPLES and TOMBS

Many of the buildings built by the Ancient Egyptians still survive today. The pyramids and tombs were places for burying people and the temples for worshipping gods.

Pyramids

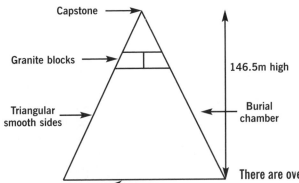

Capstone

Granite blocks

Triangular smooth sides

146.5m high

Burial chamber

Square base

The Egyptians buried their Pharaohs in a room or chamber inside the pyramid. The Great Pyramid at Giza was built for King Khufu. It is the biggest pyramid and took 100,000 men about 20 years to build.

There are over 80 pyramids still surviving in Egypt.

What did people do in temples?

Ordinary people were not allowed in the temples. The Egyptians believed temples were the homes of the gods and only the Pharaoh and his priests were allowed in them. If you visit Egypt today you can still visit ancient temples that have survived at Karnak, Luxor, Abu Simbel and Edfu. Look on a map of Egypt to find these places.

What were tombs?

Most people in Ancient Egypt were buried in the ground, but if you were rich you could afford to have a tomb. It was cut out of rock and decorated with colourful wall paintings. The most famous tomb is Tutankhamen's, which was discovered in 1922 by an archaeologist called Howard Carter.

DID YOU KNOW?

Although Tutankhamen was only 17 when he died, his tomb was full of solid gold objects including weapons, furniture, model boats and jewellery. Wow! It must have been amazing to find.

Pupil copymaster

Spidergram of the River Nile

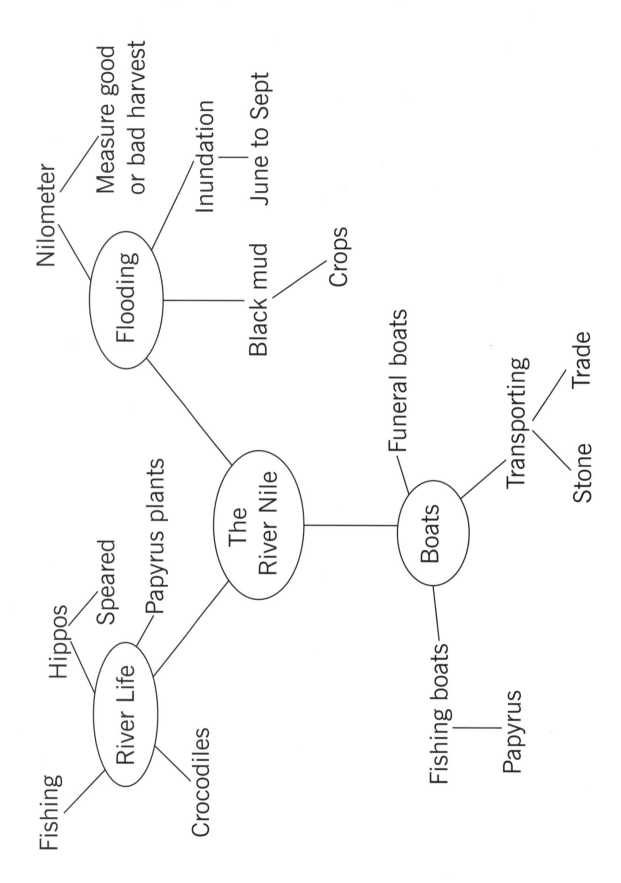

(Exemplar material)

QUAD grid on the River Nile

Question	Answer	Details	
Could you go fishing on the River Nile?	Yes. Some people had small fishing boats and they had fishing nets for catching fish.	They would also catch hippos in the River Nile by spearing them.	
What happened when the Nile flooded?	The people who lived near the river would move to higher land. The floods would leave black mud which was good for growing crops.	Some years the Nile didn't flood. This would mean a bad harvest and not enough food.	
What kind of boats went on the Nile?			

Pupil copymaster

A Nilometer

Classworks Literacy Year 3 © Carolyn Bray, Nelson Thornes Ltd 2003

(Exemplar material)

Checklists and model for non-chronological reports

Example of a checklist for non-chronological reports

- Include a heading – this could be a question

- Include subheadings – these could be questions

- Write an introductory paragraph

- Use pictures and diagrams

- Include labels and captions

- Stick to short, simple pieces of information

- Include definitions – explaining what something is

- Include facts

- Include a 'fascinating fact'

- Organise information into sections or paragraphs

- Use technical words to do with the subject

- Include a question to the reader

Example of a checklist for the first paragraph

- Use a subheading

- Write in short, simple sentences

- Use facts

- Use technical language

- Write in the past tense

- Use capital letters for proper nouns

Example of modelling a first paragraph

FLOODING THE LAND

For thousands of years the Nile flooded its banks between June and September. This was called inundation. The floodwaters deposited black mud on the river banks on which the Egyptians grew their crops. A Nilometer measured the depth of the floodwaters. If the floodwaters were not high enough it was a poor harvest and if they were too high they washed away the houses and crops.

Example of a checklist for diagrams

- Do a simple, clear line drawing

- Label with key words (not adjectives)

- Print the labels

- Draw leader lines with a ruler and make sure they are horizontal

- Write a caption to explain the diagram

(**Marking ladder**)

Name: _____

Pupil	Objective	Teacher
	I used clear, bold writing for my page title.	
	I included an introductory paragraph.	
	I included subheadings – some written as questions to interest the reader.	
	I used technical words to do with the subject.	
	I included labelled diagrams.	
	I wrote captions for pictures and diagrams.	
	I organised information into paragraphs and linked them to the categories in my spidergram.	
	I made consistent use of the past tense.	
	I included facts or pieces of information written in sentences.	
	I used only factual adjectives.	
	I used full stops and capital letters in the right places.	
	I included a question to the reader, for example, Did you know?	
	What could I do to improve my report next time?	

Traditional Stories

Outcome

An alternative version of a traditional story

Objectives

Sentence

2 [be taught] the function of adjectives within sentences, through: identifying adjectives in shared reading; discussing and defining what they have in common; i.e. words which qualify nouns; experimenting with deleting and substituting adjectives and noting effects on meaning; collecting and classifying adjectives; experimenting with the impact of different adjectives through shared writing.

3 to use the term 'adjective' appropriately.

Text

1 to investigate the styles and voices of traditional story language – collect examples, e.g. story openings and endings; scene openers: e.g. 'Now when ...', 'A long time ago'; list, compare and use in own writing.

2 to identify typical story themes, e.g. trials and forfeits, good over evil, weak over strong, wise over foolish

3 to identify and discuss main and recurring characters, evaluate their behaviour and justify views;

7 to describe and sequence key incidents in a variety of ways, e.g. by listing, charting, mapping, making simple storyboards;

9 to write a story plan for own myth, fable or traditional tale, using story theme from reading but substituting different characters or changing the setting;

10 to write alternative sequels to traditional stories using same characters and settings, identifying typical phrases and expressions from story and using these to help structure the writing.

Planning frame

- Compare modern retellings of traditional stories.

- Use structure to write own version of a traditional story.

Note

- The framework objectives refer to 'a sequel to a traditional story'. However, before the children can write a sequel to a story they need to be clear about the structure of a story that is familiar to them. Following this unit, it is perfectly feasible to plan and write a sequel to their own story or *Cinderboy*, for example, using the read/write pattern.

- Both texts in this unit have been annotated with language features such as connectives and adverbial phrases that are not in the framework objectives for this term. But as traditional stories rely heavily on these language features, it would be pedantic not to refer to them during this unit.

- This unit could be extended by giving the children an opportunity to write their traditional story by collating all their written materials.

- You will need a copy of *Cinderboy*, by Laurence Anholt, or a similar story, for this unit.

How you could plan this unit

Day 1	Day 2	Day 3	Day 4	Day 5
Reading	**Planning for writing**	**Reading**	**Writing**	**Reading** Build up of *Cinderboy*. Create checklist
Two Cinderellas	*Storyboards*	*Story Language*	*Writing an Opening*	

Day 6	Day 7	Day 8	Day 9	Day 10
Writing	**Reading** Climax (the 'magic') of *Cinderboy*. Create checklist	**Writing** Modelled and independent writing – the 'magic'	**Reading** Climax of *Cinderboy* – the action. Create checklist	**Writing** Modelled and independent writing – the action
Story Build-up				

Day 11	Day 12
Reading Resolution and traditional ending of *Cinderboy*. Create checklist	**Writing** Modelled and independent writing – resolution and ending

Two Cinderellas

Objective

We will identify the similarities in two traditional stories

You need: Resource Pages A–C, G and L.

Whole class work

- Begin by recapping with your class the story of *Cinderella*. See how much detail the children can recall.

- In pairs, the children name some traditional stories. Write these on the board.

- The children illustrate one significant event from *Cinderella*. Take feedback from one or two children.

- With your class, read *Alex and the Glass Slipper* (Resource Pages A–C). Stop at key events and discuss comparisons with *Cinderella*, using the comparison chart on Resource Page G as a basis. Begin a class checklist of similarities in basic text structure and content (refer to Resource Pages G and L):

> a goody
> baddies
> goody has to work for baddies
> goody has a wish
> some magic
> a warning or deadline
> an item or clue left behind
> goody's wish comes true
> a happy ending

Independent, pair or guided work

- The children use the planning frame (Resource Page G) to compare the stories. (Some children may use a partially completed frame for the independent time, based on ability.)

Plenary

- Use the frame to review similarities and reinforce the structure of a traditional story. ***What are some of the differences in the stories?*** The children discuss with response partners.

- ***What has the author changed to make her version of a traditional story?*** Point out change of characters and setting.

Storyboards

Objective

We will use a storyboard to plan our own traditional story using the structure of another

You need: Resource Pages H, I and L.

Whole class work

- *Today we are going to plan our own version of a traditional story by changing the characters and the setting of* Cinderella *and* Alex and the Glass Slipper, *but keeping the structure the same.*

- In pairs and using whiteboards, give the children two minutes to write as many checklist features as they can for the structure of a traditional story.

- Take feedback and compare with the class checklist from the previous lesson. Also see Resource Page L for ideas.

- Use the storyboard (Resource Page H) to demonstrate planning a traditional story. The questions are there to remind the writer of key features.

- A storyboard is usually drawn – however there may be children in your class who would either want to use words in note form or a combination of drawings and pictures. You may decide therefore to use a variety of methods when demonstrating your storyboard.

- During the demonstration ensure that you:
  - explain verbally all your thought processes and your decisions
  - give the children the 'big picture' (what is going to happen in the story in general) before planning the detail
  - reread your work or retell the story from the pictures before moving on to the next
  - do not plan each box sequentially. Story ideas do not always come in the correct sequence when planning – ensure that your planning demonstrates this
  - planning is about thinking, not about writing – ensure that you verbalise your ideas before writing them
  - write in note form (if demonstrating using a written method).

- At points in the planning process include the children in the decision-making, for example, ideas for what the deadline might be, what magic might be done and so on.

- Take feedback and explain why you have chosen one suggestion over another.

Independent, pair or guided work

- Using the blank frame (Resource Page I) or whiteboards, the children produce a storyboard of their own traditional story.

Plenary

- Using the class checklist from the previous lesson, the children check their storyboard to ensure they have used the key features.

- The children orally rehearse elements of their story with response partners. For example, *Tell your partner who is going to do the magic in your story. What are the names of the baddies? What are the baddies invited to?*

Story Language

Objective

We will find out what language features authors use for the opening of a traditional story

You need: Resource Pages A (one copy per child), D, G, J and L; flip chart.

Whole class work

- Read together the opening of *Cinderboy* (Resource Page J). Discuss briefly any similarities with *Alex and the Glass Slipper* or *Cinderella*. (You could use the completed comparison frame from a previous lesson to focus discussion.)

- In pairs, ask the following kinds of questions to begin building a class checklist for the opening of a traditional story (see Resource Page L for ideas):
  - *What do we learn about the characters from the opening of the story?*
  - *What words describe the characters?* (Introduce the term 'adjective'.)
  - *What does Cinderboy have to do for his brothers and dad?*

- Identify the checklist features in the text.

Independent, pair or guided work

- The children annotate copies of the opening of *Alex and the Glass Slipper* (Resource Page A) to show checklist features they have identified.

Plenary

- Display Resource Page D for the whole class to agree checklist features.

- Experiment with replacing adjectives with alternatives to change the meaning of the text.

- In pairs, the children write two or three adjectives on their whiteboards and reread the sentence, replacing original adjectives with alternatives. For example:

> Alex was a lazy and sloppy worker.

Writing an Opening

Objective

We will write the opening of our own traditional story using the correct language features and structures

You need: Resource Pages H, K and L; whiteboards; coloured pens or highlighters.

Whole class work

- In pairs, the children find three things they have learnt about openings for a traditional story. Take feedback.

- Refer back to the Kylie storyboard (Resource Page H). With the children, review the characters to be introduced.

- In pairs and using whiteboards, the children write two adjectives for the brothers and two adjectives for Kylie. Take some feedback and ask the children why they have chosen particular adjectives.

- Model writing the opening of your story (Resource Page K), ensuring that you:
  - refer back to the storyboard
  - rehearse the sentences orally before putting them on to paper
  - experiment with alternative adjectives to describe the characters
  - remind the children to use the checklist
  - ask the children to indicate when they think you have used something on the checklist
  - involve your class in contributing some ideas, for example, 'What kind of jobs do you think Kylie might have to do at home?'

Independent, pair or guided work

- Each child chooses two adjectives to describe the 'goody' in their story. On whiteboards, the children write their opening sentence including these adjectives, for example:

  > Scott was a happy, hardworking boy who could swim like a fish.

- The children use the example of your demonstration writing and the checklist on Resource Page L to write the opening of their own traditional story.

- Remind the children to rehearse the sentence in their head before writing it down, as you demonstrated in your writing.

- It is often more successful to allow the children to compose on a whiteboard at this point. The transient nature of work done on a whiteboard often means that even reluctant writers are happy to give it a go – as it can always be rubbed off. Photocopy the whiteboards at the end of the session for evidence.

Plenary

- Using different coloured pens or highlighters, the children underline where they have used the features identified on the checklist in their writing. For example: adjectives to describe the goody and baddies could be underlined in red, jobs done by the goody in green and so on. This allows the children to 'mark' their own work and you to assess their level of understanding and their application of the language features.

Story Build-up

Objective

We will write the build-up of our own traditional story using the correct language features and structures

You need: Resource Pages H, K and L; OHTs.

Whole class work

- Review the checklist for a story build-up (checklist 2, Resource Page L). Refer the children to the storyboard (Resource Page H) to remind them what is going to happen in this part of the story.

- In pairs, the children discuss what is going to happen in their own story during build-up.

- Demonstrate writing a build-up (for example, Resource Page K). Ensure that you:
  - refer to the storyboard
  - rehearse sentences orally before writing
  - refer to the checklist – ask the children to indicate when they think you have used something on the checklist
  - discuss the choice of words used, for example, powerful verbs following speech
  - remind the children of the rules for writing speech.

- Use role play during the demonstration writing to develop the conversation between the characters. Select three children to play the main characters and ask the class to suggest what they would say to each other and how they would say it.

Independent, pair or guided work

- Using checklist 2 on Resource Page L and your modelled writing as support, the children write their own build-up based on their plan.

- Select one or two children to work on an OHT for use in the plenary.

Plenary

- Check the work produced on the OHT against the checklist features. Focus on the powerful verbs following the speech. ***What do they tell us about the characters?***

- The children check their own work against the checklist.

(**Pupil copymaster**)

Alex and the Glass Slipper – introduction and build-up

Alex was the kitchenhand at The Flinders' Cellar restaurant. He was a hard and honest worker and it was not long before the chefs, Manuel and Russell Flinders, took advantage of this. Instead of just peeling vegetables and washing dishes, Alex was made to do the shopping, wash and press the two chefs' uniforms and clean the restaurant from top to bottom every day.

Soon the chefs became so lazy that they made Alex cook all the meals for the guests by himself, while they took all the credit.

"What wonderful pumpkin soup, Russell," remarked one customer.

"Fabulously fluffy mousse, Manuel," commented another.

"It's not fair!" said Alex to himself.

One day, in the afternoon mail, Manuel and Russell received a letter from the king's palace announcing 'The Royal Cake-Baking Contest'.

"Alex, you will bake the cakes for us," demanded Russell.

When Alex had finished baking, the chefs were overjoyed.

"I think my strawberry sponge will win," said Manuel.

"No, my iced jubilee cake will," said Russell. "It's a pity Alex can't cook or he could come, too!" Both chefs screeched with laughter. Alex felt like putting his feet through the cakes, but he needed his job, so he didn't.

"It's not fair," complained Alex when the two chefs had gone. "I have to run the restaurant while those two take my cakes to the contest."

"I can look after the place," offered Polly Goodfellow, the waiter. "You bake your best cheesecake and I'll take care of everything else."

Amanda Graham, in The Magic Bean Big Book

(**Pupil copymaster**)

Alex and the Glass Slipper – climax (magic and action)

While Alex looked in his secret cookbook for his special recipe, Polly opened a secret book of her own – a book of magic.

"It's finished!" Alex soon announced. "My cheesecake looks great, but what about me? I can't go to the competition dressed like a kitchenhand!"

"Open the cupboard," suggested Polly calmly. To Alex's amazement, inside the cupboard was a neatly pressed chef's uniform, a tall chef's hat and pair of shiny, black shoes – all in his size.

"Now open the back door," said Polly.

Outside the restaurant where he had left his old pushbike early that morning, was a shiny red motorcycle.

"Wow! Thanks, Polly!" exclaimed Alex. "You're magic!"

"Now remember," warned Polly, "you must return by midnight, for then the magic ends. Remember, Alex! Remember!"

When Alex arrived at the palace, the princess, the king and the royal chef had already begun the judging.

"Exquisite!" remarked the royal chef as he tasted Manuel's sponge.

"Magnificent!" the king said of Russell's iced jubilee. "It seems we have the winners here."

"Wait, we haven't tried this one," called out the beautiful princess.

Each judge tasted a piece of Alex's cheesecake. As the princess swallowed the last bite she gazed into Alex's eyes. The man who could cook like this was the man she wanted to marry.

"We have a winner," announced the king. "Number 84!" It was Alex! The princess stepped forward to present the prize. Just at that moment a clock began to strike twelve. Alex panicked and fled into the night. Outside he found that his shiny motorbike had changed back into a rusty old pushbike with a flat tyre.

"Ah well," sighed Alex, in his old kitchen clothes, "it was nice while it lasted."

Amanda Graham, in The Magic Bean Big Book

Alex and the Glass Slipper – resolution and ending

The princess could not forget Alex and his cheesecake. The next day she made a proclamation that she loved the chef who had won the contest and wanted to present his prize personally.

She sent the royal chef to all the restaurants to find Alex. Eventually, the chef knocked on the door of The Flinders' Cellar.

"Come in," said Russell, "and try the cheesecakes that Manuel and I have baked." (Really Alex had baked them but of course he had not used his special recipe.)

"It's chocolatey," said the royal chef, "but not quite ..."

"... chocolatey enough?" chimed Alex. "Try this one!"

Manuel and Russell laughed. "He's only the kitchenhand."

The royal chef looked carefully at Alex. Had he seen him somewhere before?

Slowly, the chef tasted a piece of Alex's cake. He recognised that special flavour at once.

"This is it!" he squealed with delight. "I have found the mystery chef. Inform the princess at once!"

The princess was promptly driven to the restaurant to congratulate Alex.

"Here is your prize," said the beautiful princess, kissing Alex lightly on the cheek. "Will you marry me and cook for me forever?"

"Oh, thank you, your Highness," said Alex, surprised, "but I already have a partner."

The princess was astonished. The room was silent. How could Alex refuse such a proposal?

"Polly's been such a good friend," he said. "The two of us have decided to start up our own restaurant. We'll call it 'The Glass Slipper'."

And that's just what they did and they worked and lived ... happily ever after.

Amanda Graham, in The Magic Bean Big Book

(Exemplar analysis)

Example of analysis of *Alex and the Glass Slipper* – *introduction and build-up*

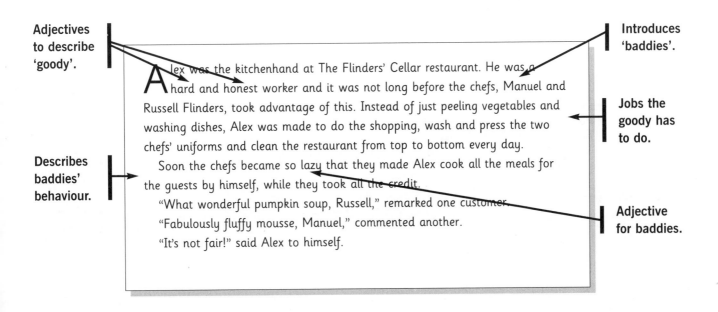

Adjectives to describe 'goody'.

Describes baddies' behaviour.

Introduces 'baddies'.

Jobs the goody has to do.

Adjective for baddies.

Alex was the kitchenhand at The Flinders' Cellar restaurant. He was a hard and honest worker and it was not long before the chefs, Manuel and Russell Flinders, took advantage of this. Instead of just peeling vegetables and washing dishes, Alex was made to do the shopping, wash and press the two chefs' uniforms and clean the restaurant from top to bottom every day.

Soon the chefs became so lazy that they made Alex cook all the meals for the guests by himself, while they took all the credit.

"What wonderful pumpkin soup, Russell," remarked one customer.

"Fabulously fluffy mousse, Manuel," commented another.

"It's not fair!" said Alex to himself.

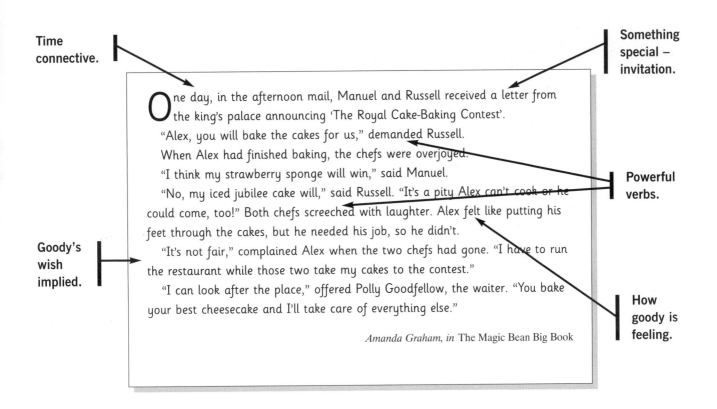

Time connective.

Goody's wish implied.

Something special – invitation.

Powerful verbs.

How goody is feeling.

One day, in the afternoon mail, Manuel and Russell received a letter from the king's palace announcing 'The Royal Cake-Baking Contest'.

"Alex, you will bake the cakes for us," demanded Russell.

When Alex had finished baking, the chefs were overjoyed.

"I think my strawberry sponge will win," said Manuel.

"No, my iced jubilee cake will," said Russell. "It's a pity Alex can't cook or he could come, too!" Both chefs screeched with laughter. Alex felt like putting his feet through the cakes, but he needed his job, so he didn't.

"It's not fair," complained Alex when the two chefs had gone. "I have to run the restaurant while those two take my cakes to the contest."

"I can look after the place," offered Polly Goodfellow, the waiter. "You bake your best cheesecake and I'll take care of everything else."

Amanda Graham, in The Magic Bean Big Book

(Pupil copymaster)

Example of analysis of *Alex and the Glass Slipper* – climax (magic and action)

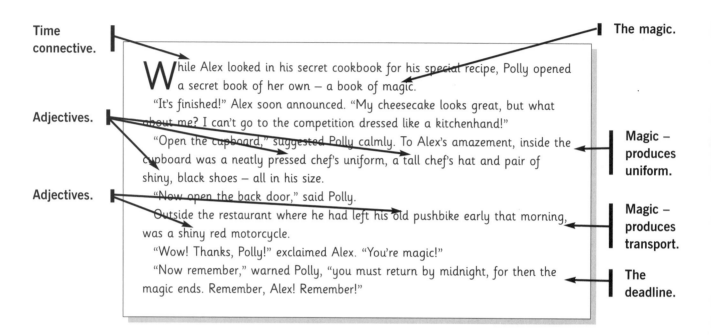

Time connective.

The magic.

While Alex looked in his secret cookbook for his special recipe, Polly opened a secret book of her own – a book of magic.

"It's finished!" Alex soon announced. "My cheesecake looks great, but what about me? I can't go to the competition dressed like a kitchenhand!"

Adjectives.

"Open the cupboard," suggested Polly calmly. To Alex's amazement, inside the cupboard was a neatly pressed chef's uniform, a tall chef's hat and pair of shiny, black shoes – all in his size.

Magic – produces uniform.

Adjectives.

"Now open the back door," said Polly.

Outside the restaurant where he had left his old pushbike early that morning, was a shiny red motorcycle.

Magic – produces transport.

"Wow! Thanks, Polly!" exclaimed Alex. "You're magic!"

"Now remember," warned Polly, "you must return by midnight, for then the magic ends. Remember, Alex! Remember!"

The deadline.

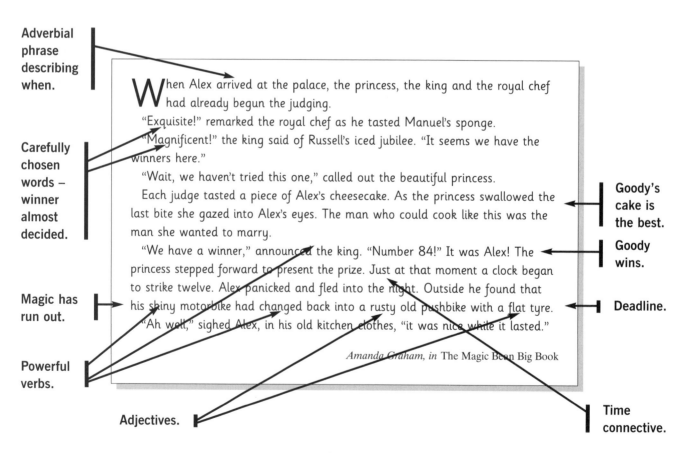

Adverbial phrase describing when.

When Alex arrived at the palace, the princess, the king and the royal chef had already begun the judging.

"Exquisite!" remarked the royal chef as he tasted Manuel's sponge.

Carefully chosen words – winner almost decided.

"Magnificent!" the king said of Russell's iced jubilee. "It seems we have the winners here."

"Wait, we haven't tried this one," called out the beautiful princess.

Each judge tasted a piece of Alex's cheesecake. As the princess swallowed the last bite she gazed into Alex's eyes. The man who could cook like this was the man she wanted to marry.

Goody's cake is the best.

Goody wins.

"We have a winner," announced the king. "Number 84!" It was Alex! The princess stepped forward to present the prize. Just at that moment a clock began to strike twelve. Alex panicked and fled into the night. Outside he found that his shiny motorbike had changed back into a rusty old pushbike with a flat tyre.

Magic has run out.

Deadline.

"Ah well," sighed Alex, in his old kitchen clothes, "it was nice while it lasted."

Powerful verbs.

Amanda Graham, in The Magic Bean Big Book

Adjectives.

Time connective.

(Exemplar analysis)

Example of analysis of *Alex and The Glass Slipper* – *resolution and ending*

Traditional story language.

Time connectives.

Someone sent to find Alex.

Brackets for extra details.

Baddies' cakes are tried – not quite right.

Adverb.

Question.

Powerful verbs.

Adverbial phrase.

Adverbs.

Prize finally given to goody.

Question.

Twist at end – goody does not want prize! – but gets better prize.

Wish has come true.

Traditional ending.

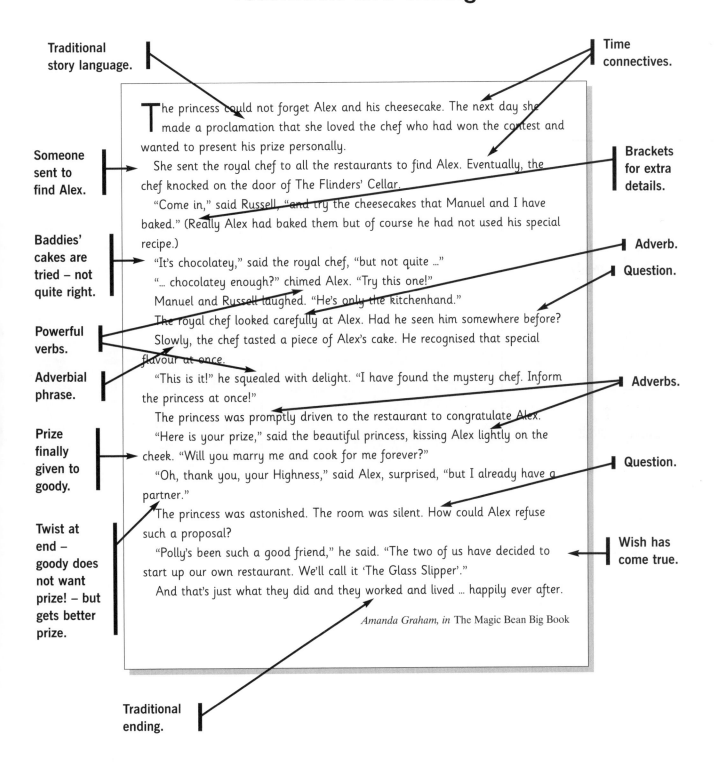

The princess could not forget Alex and his cheesecake. The next day she made a proclamation that she loved the chef who had won the contest and wanted to present his prize personally.

She sent the royal chef to all the restaurants to find Alex. Eventually, the chef knocked on the door of The Flinders' Cellar.

"Come in," said Russell, "and try the cheesecakes that Manuel and I have baked." (Really Alex had baked them but of course he had not used his special recipe.)

"It's chocolatey," said the royal chef, "but not quite …"

"… chocolatey enough?" chimed Alex. "Try this one!"

Manuel and Russell laughed. "He's only the kitchenhand."

The royal chef looked carefully at Alex. Had he seen him somewhere before? Slowly, the chef tasted a piece of Alex's cake. He recognised that special flavour at once.

"This is it!" he squealed with delight. "I have found the mystery chef. Inform the princess at once!"

The princess was promptly driven to the restaurant to congratulate Alex.

"Here is your prize," said the beautiful princess, kissing Alex lightly on the cheek. "Will you marry me and cook for me forever?"

"Oh, thank you, your Highness," said Alex, surprised, "but I already have a partner."

The princess was astonished. The room was silent. How could Alex refuse such a proposal?

"Polly's been such a good friend," he said. "The two of us have decided to start up our own restaurant. We'll call it 'The Glass Slipper'."

And that's just what they did and they worked and lived … happily ever after.

Amanda Graham, in The Magic Bean Big Book

Planning frame for comparing stories

	Alex and the Glass Slipper	*Cinderella*
Goody		
Baddy		
Jobs for goody		
Invitation		
Goody's wish		
Who does the magic?		
What is the warning?		
What is left behind?		
How does the wish come true?		

Pupil copymaster

Kylie storyboard

Opening – Introduction of characters, goody and baddies

Josh and Ryan – brothers, love skateboarding. Kylie – stepsister. Loves skateboarding, but has to do vacuuming, their homework. Has only got very old skateboard thrown out by brothers.

Build-up – Invite and wish

Skateboard competition. Kylie must stay at home and repair the spare skateboards and polish their trophies.

Climax – the action (What does the goody do? How does he/she know the time has run out? What does he/she leave behind?

No one recognises her because of helmet. She scores highest points in the competition. Hears watch alarm. Runs and leaves helmet in the changing room.

Climax – the magic (Who does the magic? What is turned into what? What's the warning or deadline?)

Wizard zooms in on skateboard. Vacuum turns into skateboard, baseball cap into helmet, dusters and cloths into knee and elbow pads. Must be home by 6pm – sets alarm on her watch.

Resolution and ending (How is the goody found? What is the prize? How does it end?)

Judges come to house to see who will fit the helmet, so they can give trophy and prize of brand new hi-tech skateboard and accessories. Helmet fits Kylie. Kylie lets brothers use new skateboard occasionally and they all go to competitions together.

Pupil copymaster

Blank storyboard

Opening – Introduction of characters, goody and baddies

Build-up – Invite and wish (What is the invitation for? What does the goody wish for?)

Climax – the magic (Who does the magic? What is turned into what? What's the warning or deadline?)

Climax – the action (What does the goody do? How does he/she know the time has run out? What does he/she leave behind?)

Resolution and ending (How is the goody found? What is the prize? How does it end?)

(**Pupil copymaster**)

Cinderboy – introduction

Cinderboy was crazy about football. His wicked stepdad and his two lazy stepbrothers were football crazy too. The whole family supported Royal Palace United.

Every Saturday they would lie about on the sofa with the remote control and watch their favourite team on TV. Royal Palace always played brilliantly in their smart pink shorts and shirts.

But not poor Cinderboy. He wasn't even allowed to watch. He had to wait on his stepbrothers hand and foot, and bring them cups of tea and bowl after bowl of peanuts, which were their favourite snack.

Cinderboy's family was very noisy and bad mannered. When Royal Palace scored they would jump up and down on the sofa and shout for more peanuts to celebrate.

And when the other team scored they would throw their peanuts at the TV, then yell at Cinderboy to pick them up so that they could throw them again.

Laurence Anholt

(Exemplar material)

Modelled writing

OPENING

Kylie was a kind, cheerful girl who was crazy about skateboarding. Her two miserable, selfish step-brothers, Josh and Ryan, were also crazy about skateboarding. Every day, after school, they would take their brand new boards to the park and practise jumping off ramps, pivoting, turning and sliding along pipes.

While they were out having fun, poor Kylie had to stay at home to vacuum their bedrooms, do their homework and cook their tea. If ever she did go out to play then all she had was a very old, wobbly, rusty skateboard that had been thrown away by Ryan.

BUILD-UP

One day a leaflet was posted through their front door advertising a skateboard competition.

"We're entering the competition," announced Josh.

"And I am going to win!" boasted Ryan.

"I'd like to come. Can I borrow a skateboard?" Kylie asked nervously.

"No way!" snapped Josh.

"While we are away you must patch our kneepads, oil the wheels on our spare boards and polish our trophies until they shine like the sun," ordered Ryan.

Poor Kylie was so unhappy. She loved skateboarding and wanted to enter the competition more than anything in the world, especially as the first prize was a fabulous new skateboard with all the accessories.

(Exemplar material)

Checklists for traditional stories

Example of a checklist for writing the introduction ①

- Use a traditional opening
- Introduce characters: goody, baddies
- Use adjectives to describe characters
- Describe what the character is made to do

(Neither *Cinderboy* nor *Alex and the Glass Slipper* has a traditional opening such as 'Once upon a time'. This is because both are modern versions. However you may wish to include this on the checklist.)

Example of a checklist for writing the build-up ②

- Use a time connective, for example, 'one day'
- Include an invitation – baddies go, not goody
- Include a speech – orders for goody
- Use further time connectives, for example, 'the next morning'
- Describe the wish of goody

Example of a checklist for writing the climax (magic) ③

- Use time connectives, for example, 'Suddenly'
- Introduce magic character with speech
- Use adverbial phrases, for example, 'as if by magic'
- Magic provides clothes and transport
- Include a warning or deadline, for example, return by midnight

Example of a checklist for writing the climax (action) ④

- Use a time connective, for example, 'It seemed like only seconds'
- Use powerful verbs to describe what goody is doing
- Goody wins
- Time runs out – use a time connective, for example, 'Just at that moment, as the clock struck 12'
- Magic runs out
- A clue is left, for example, shoe

Example of a checklist for writing the resolution ⑤

- Use time connectives, for example, 'the next morning', 'a few days later'
- Speech should introduce baddies trying on the clue left behind (glass slipper)
- Goody's wish comes true

Example of a checklist for writing the ending ⑥

- Goody forgives baddies
- They all live happily ever after

Classworks Literacy Year 3 © Carolyn Bray, Nelson Thornes Ltd 2003

(Marking ladder)

Name: _____

Pupil	Objective	Teacher
	I used a traditional opening.	
	I used adjectives to describe the characters.	
	I used time connectives to move on to the next part of the story.	
	I used speech to: • tell the reader what jobs the goody has to do • introduce the 'magic' character • describe the baddies trying on the 'item'.	
	I included magic and a warning.	
	I invented an item that the goody leaves behind.	
	I included a traditional ending.	
	What could I do to improve my story next time?	

Oral and Performance Poetry

Outcome

An additional verse for a known poem, to be written and performed

Objectives	**Text** **11** to write new or extended verses for performance based on models of 'performance' and oral poetry read, e.g. rhythms, repetition.
Planning frame	● Read at least two different rap poems. ● Understand the difference between poems that can be read and those that are written to be performed. ● Write and perform additional verses for rap poems.
Note	● This unit covers six days. You may wish to extend it by looking at other poems for the children to perform. Examples of poets writing in this way include Valerie Bloom, Grace Nichols, John Agard, Fred D'Aguiar and James Berry. Raps appropriate for classroom use include *Write-A-Rap Rap* by Tony Mitton, and *I Luv Me Mudder* by Benjamin Zephaniah.

How you could plan this unit

Day 1	Day 2	Day 3	Day 4	Day 5
Reading	Speaking and Listening	Writing	Writing Demonstrate writing lines 3 and 4	Writing Demonstrate writing chorus
Two Raps	*Performing to an Audience*	*Writing Rap*		

Day 6
Speaking and listening Class performance of new verses

Two Raps

Objective

We will investigate how a poet writes a rap, so we can write and perform our own

You need: Resource Pages A–E; a percussion instrument.

Whole class work

- Read aloud *Gran, Can You Rap?* (Resource Page A), demonstrating the rhythm and beat. Ask the children to join in reading aloud one verse at a time, checking for the rhythm and beat.

- Use a percussion instrument played by you or a child to keep the beat as you read the poem aloud.

- In pairs, the children discuss the text by telling their response partner which verse they liked the best and why. ***Do you think it is funny? Why?***

- Ask the children to picture 'Gran' (or their own gran) rapping. Read the poem aloud again, as they picture the actions in the poem.

- Begin building a checklist of the language and text features of the poem (see Resource Page E for ideas). Prompt the children by asking:

> Does this poem rhyme?
>
> Where does it rhyme?
>
> What do you notice at the beginning of each line?
>
> What can you tell me about the words in the last line of the chorus?

Independent, pair or guided work

- The children identify and highlight checklist features in *The Schoolkids' Rap* (Resource Pages C and D).

Plenary

- Draw up a chart of similarities and differences between the two poems to draw out the language features.

- Read *The Schoolkids' Rap* aloud. In pairs the children discuss which poem they prefer and why.

- ***Why are these poems better read aloud than in your head?***

Performing to an Audience

Objective

We will prepare and give a performance of a poem

You need: Resource Pages A–E; a percussion instrument; other rap poems
(see introductory note).

Whole class work

- Reinforce the idea that these types of poems are written to be performed to an audience, not just read.

- Demonstrate reading *Gran, Can You Rap?* (Resource Page A) in a narrative style without clear intonation or volume. Ask the children to discuss whether or not it was a good performance.

- Discuss the importance of rhythm, beat, volume and clear pronunciation. Begin to produce a checklist for rap performance (see checklist 2, Resource Page E for ideas).

- Bear in mind that some children may not like performing in front of others, or may have speech impediments. These children could 'perform' their raps by recording on to tape or video.

- Perform the first verse of the poem as a class, checking for rhythm, beat, volume and clarity.

- You might want to include the use of a percussion instrument to reinforce the rhythm.

- *What other things do we need to remember when performing a rap?* Allow the children to think about using actions – this is particularly valuable for the kinaesthetic learners. *What actions do you think would go with this rap?* Take some feedback.

Independent, pair or guided work

- The children work in pairs or small groups to prepare a performance of one verse of *Gran, Can You Rap?* or *The Schoolkids' Rap* (Resource Page C), using the class checklist as a guide. Children who do not like speaking in front of others could still do the actions.

Plenary

- The children perform their verse of the rap to the rest of the class. Use the checklist as a guide and encourage the children to comment using a response sandwich: one good comment, one idea for improvement, another good comment.

- To enable all the children to perform, this plenary will have to be much longer than usual.

71

Writing a Rap

Objective

We will write two lines of a new verse for *Gran, Can You Rap?*

You need: Resource Pages A and E.

Whole class work

- Briefly review *Gran, Can You Rap?* (Resource Page A) by reading it again.

- In pairs, the children brainstorm three of the points from the class checklist for writing a rap poem (Resource Page E, checklist 1). Take feedback.

- Explain that they are going to use *Gran, Can you Rap?* and the class checklist to write the first two lines of a new verse for the rap. In this shared writing session you will model an example so the children can practise on whiteboards. This will give plenty of ideas for their independent work later.

- *Where might Gran rap?* Brainstorm ideas with your class about places Gran could rap. In pairs, the children come up with three places.

- Select a word to go at the end of the first line, for example, 'school'. Orally demonstrate that the rap has rhyming words and that you will have to find a word to rhyme at the end of the second line. The children select one or two words from their list of places and write the rhyme on their whiteboards.

- Demonstrate writing the first line:

> She rapped in the park and she rapped at school.

The children check the writing against the checklist.

- Decide on a word for the end of the second line that rhymes with the end of the first line, for example, 'pool'. The children do the same for their rap.

- Demonstrate checking for rhythm, rhyme and the other features on the checklist as you write the second line:

> She rapped round the field and she rapped round the pool.

- The rhyming work gives you the opportunity to discuss long vowel phonemes and the various combinations of letters that make the same phoneme, for example, 'night', 'kite', 'height'.

Independent, pair or guided work

- The children work in pairs to draft at least one idea for the first two lines (see Resource Page E for ideas for remodelling whole verse).

Plenary

- Selected children 'perform' their two lines and the class evaluate the lines using the checklist and a response sandwich: one good comment, one idea for improvement, another good comment.

(Pupil copymaster)

Gran, Can You Rap?

Gran was in her chair she was taking a nap
When I tapped her on the shoulder to see if she could rap.
Gran, can you rap? Can you rap? Can you, Gran?
And she opened one eye and she said to me, Man,
I'm the best rapping Gran this world's ever seen
I'm a tip-top, slip-slap, rap-rap queen.

And she rose from her chair in the corner of the room
And she started to rap with a bim-bam-boom,
And she rolled up her eyes and she rolled round her head
And as she rolled by this is what she said,
I'm the best rapping Gran this world's ever seen
I'm a nip-nap, yip-yap, rap-rap queen.

Then she rapped past my dad and she rapped past my mother,
She rapped past me and my little baby brother.
She rapped her arms narrow she rapped her arms wide,
She rapped through the door and she rapped outside.
She's the best rapping Gran this world's ever seen
She's a drip-drop, trip-trap, rap-rap queen.

She rapped down the garden she rapped down the street,
The neighbours all cheered and they tapped their feet.
She rapped through the traffic lights as they turned red
As she rapped round the corner this is what she said,
I'm the best rapping Gran this world's ever seen
I'm a flip-flop, hip-hop, rap-rap queen.

She rapped down the lane she rapped up the hill,
And as she disappeared she was rapping still.
I could hear Gran's voice saying, Listen, Man,
Listen to the rapping of the rap-rap Gran.
I'm the best rapping Gran this world's ever seen
I'm a –
    tip-top, slip-slap,
       nip-nap, yip-yap,
         hip-hop, trip-trap
          touch yer cap,
           take a nap,
            happy, happy, happy, happy,
             rap—rap—queen.

Jack Ousbey

Classworks Literacy Year 3 © Carolyn Bray, Nelson Thornes Ltd 2003

(Exemplar analysis)

Example of analysis of *Gran, Can You Rap?*

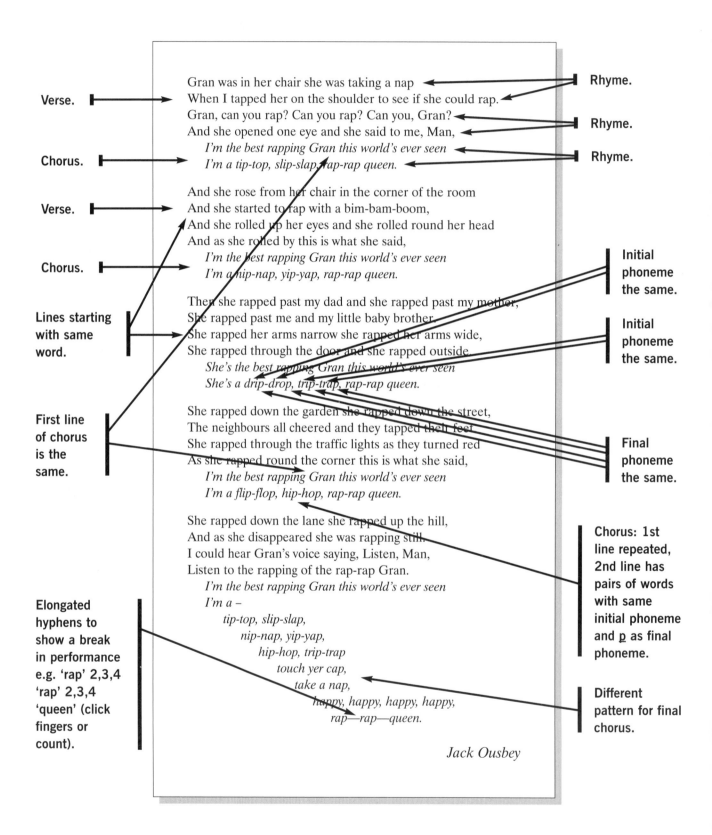

Verse.

Gran was in her chair she was taking a nap — **Rhyme.**
When I tapped her on the shoulder to see if she could rap.
Gran, can you rap? Can you rap? Can you, Gran? — **Rhyme.**
And she opened one eye and she said to me, Man,

Chorus.

I'm the best rapping Gran this world's ever seen — **Rhyme.**
I'm a tip-top, slip-slap, rap-rap queen.

Verse.

And she rose from her chair in the corner of the room
And she started to rap with a bim-bam-boom,
And she rolled up her eyes and she rolled round her head
And as she rolled by this is what she said,

Chorus.

I'm the best rapping Gran this world's ever seen
I'm a nip-nap, yip-yap, rap-rap queen.

Lines starting with same word.

Then she rapped past my dad and she rapped past my mother,
She rapped past me and my little baby brother,
She rapped her arms narrow she rapped her arms wide,
She rapped through the door and she rapped outside.
She's the best rapping Gran this world's ever seen
She's a drip-drop, trip-trap, rap-rap queen.

Initial phoneme the same.

Initial phoneme the same.

First line of chorus is the same.

She rapped down the garden she rapped down the street,
The neighbours all cheered and they tapped their feet,
She rapped through the traffic lights as they turned red
As she rapped round the corner this is what she said,
I'm the best rapping Gran this world's ever seen
I'm a flip-flop, hip-hop, rap-rap queen.

Final phoneme the same.

She rapped down the lane she rapped up the hill,
And as she disappeared she was rapping still.
I could hear Gran's voice saying, Listen, Man,
Listen to the rapping of the rap-rap Gran.
I'm the best rapping Gran this world's ever seen
I'm a –
  tip-top, slip-slap,
    nip-nap, yip-yap,
      hip-hop, trip-trap
        touch yer cap,
          take a nap,
            happy, happy, happy, happy,
              rap—rap—queen.

Chorus: 1st line repeated, 2nd line has pairs of words with same initial phoneme and p as final phoneme.

Elongated hyphens to show a break in performance e.g. 'rap' 2,3,4 'rap' 2,3,4 'queen' (click fingers or count).

Different pattern for final chorus.

Jack Ousbey

(Pupil copymaster)

The Schoolkids' Rap

Miss was at the blackboard writing with the chalk,
When suddenly she stopped in the middle of her talk.
She snapped her fingers – snap! snap! snap!
Pay attention children and I'll teach you how to rap.

She picked up a pencil, she started to tap.
All together children, now clap! clap! clap!
Just get the rhythm, just get the beat.
Drum it with your fingers, stamp it with your feet.

That's right children, keep in time.
Now we've got the rhythm, all we need is the rhyme.
This school is cool. Miss Grace is ace.
Strut your stuff with a smile on your face.

Snap those fingers, tap those toes.
Do it like they do it on the video shows.
Flap it! Slap it! Clap! Snap! Clap!
Let's all do the schoolkids' rap!

John Foster

(Exemplar analysis)

Example of analysis of *The Schoolkids' Rap*

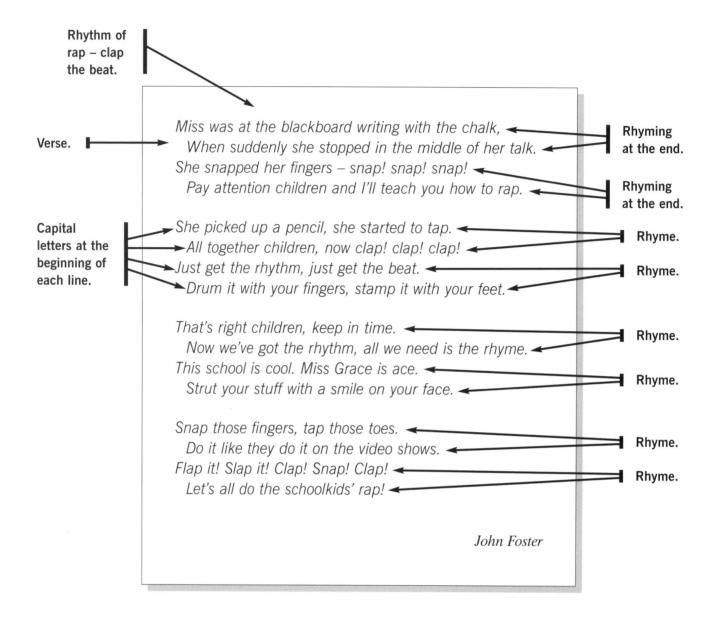

Rhythm of rap – clap the beat.

Verse.

Capital letters at the beginning of each line.

Miss was at the blackboard writing with the chalk,
When suddenly she stopped in the middle of her talk.
She snapped her fingers – snap! snap! snap!
Pay attention children and I'll teach you how to rap.

She picked up a pencil, she started to tap.
All together children, now clap! clap! clap!
Just get the rhythm, just get the beat.
Drum it with your fingers, stamp it with your feet.

That's right children, keep in time.
Now we've got the rhythm, all we need is the rhyme.
This school is cool. Miss Grace is ace.
Strut your stuff with a smile on your face.

Snap those fingers, tap those toes.
Do it like they do it on the video shows.
Flap it! Slap it! Clap! Snap! Clap!
Let's all do the schoolkids' rap!

John Foster

Rhyming at the end.

Rhyming at the end.

Rhyme.

Rhyme.

Rhyme.

Rhyme.

Rhyme.

Rhyme.

Exemplar material

Checklists and models for oral and performance poetry

Example of a checklist for writing a rap poem

- Use a strong rap rhythm/beat
- Rhyming should be in pairs at the end of every line (couplet)
- Use verses or stanzas
- Include choruses
- Use a capital letter at the beginning of every line
- First line of the chorus is always repeated
- The same opening phrase can be used in some verses
- Use pairs of words with the same initial phoneme in the chorus (e.g. 'flip-flop')
- Use words with the same final phoneme in the chorus

Example of a checklist for a rap performance

- Look at the audience
- Keep the correct rhythm
- Use a percussion instrument, clap or tap fingers to keep the rhythm
- Perform at the right speed (note: raps are quite fast)
- Take note of the punctuation
- Speak clearly and with good volume
- Use expression to make it interesting for the audience
- Use simple actions

Modelled writing – where did Gran rap?

She rapped in the park and she rapped at school.
She rapped round the field and she rapped round the pool.

Modelled writing – when did Gran rap?

She rapped all night and she rapped all day,
She rapped before lunch and she rapped after play.

Modelled writing – Gran rap chorus

She's the best rapping Gran this world's ever seen
She's a bip-bop, snip-snap, rap-rap queen.

(**Marking ladder**)

Name: _____

Pupil	Objective	Teacher
	My poem has the rhythm of a rap.	
	It has a rhyme at the end of every line.	
	It has the same opening phrase on every line.	
	I used a verse and a chorus.	
	I used a capital letter at the beginning of every line.	
	I included pairs of words in the chorus with the same initial phoneme and p̲ as the final phoneme.	
	What could I do to improve my poem next time?	

Marking ladder

Name: _____

Pupil	Objective	Teacher
	When I performed my poem I kept the strong rap rhythm.	
	I used an instrument or clapping to keep the beat.	
	I took note of the punctuation.	
	I used good expression.	
	I performed it at the right speed.	
	I pronounced all the words clearly.	
	I performed with the right amount of volume.	
	I used actions to make the performance more interesting.	
	I looked at the audience (if appropriate).	
	I smiled and enjoy performing.	
	What could I do to improve my performance next time?	

Myths

Outcome

A myth planned and written by ourselves

Objectives

Sentence

2 [be taught] the function of adjectives within sentences, through: identifying adjectives in shared reading; discussing and defining what they have in common; experimenting with deleting and substituting adjectives and noting effects on meaning; collecting and classifying adjectives; experimenting with the impact of different adjectives through shared writing.

3 to use the term 'adjective' appropriately.

6 to note where commas occur in reading and to discuss their functions in helping the reader.

7 to use the term 'comma' appropriately in relation to reading.

Text

1 to investigate the styles and voices of traditional story language – collect examples, e.g. story openings and endings; scene openers; list, compare and use in own writing.

6 to plan main points as a structure for story writing, considering how to capture points in a few words that can be elaborated later; discuss different methods of planning.

9 to write a story plan for own myth, fable or traditional tale, using story theme from reading but substituting different characters or changing the setting.

Planning frame

- Read examples of myths and identify structure and features.
- Write own myth based on this structure.

Note

- This unit makes use of speech to develop characters. Although punctuation of speech is not explicitly mentioned until Term 3, many children may be ready to use it. A lesson on speech punctuation may be inserted between Days 3 and 4 in preparation.

How you could plan this unit

Day 1	Day 2	Day 3	Day 4	Day 5
Reading	Writing	Reading	Writing	Reading
Features of Myths	*Planning for Writing*	*The Opening*	*Writing an Opening*	*The Build-up*

Day 6	Day 7	Day 8	Day 9	Day 10
Writing Use of commas, for example, before the conjunction 'but'	Writing *Writing the Build-up*	Reading Read myth climax and make a checklist	Writing Climax	Reading Resolution. Make a checklist

Day 11	Day 12	Day 13	Day 14	Day 14 (cont.)
Writing Resolution	Reading Ending. Make a checklist	Writing Ending	Writing Extended writing of complete myth. Ensure that the children use checklists and marking ladder when completing piece of	extended writing. Can be continued to Day 15 if required

Features of Myths

Objective

We will familiarise ourselves with the features of myths

You need: Resource Pages A–F and P; whiteboards and pens; flip chart.

Whole class work

- Introduce the objective and discuss the word 'myth'. *A myth is a story that would have been told (not written) in order to explain natural phenomena.*

- Give some examples of natural phenomena, for example, thunder and lightning, rainbows, earthquakes and so on.

- Read together *Rainbow Bird* (Resource Pages A and B).

- Children with SEN will benefit from having the text read to them before the lesson.

- Use questions to highlight the overall structure of the myth. *What is the myth explaining? Who are the main characters? Which words does the author use to open the myth?* Annotate the text (see Resource Pages C and D) with the features identified by the children and use them to make a checklist of the features of a myth (see checklist 1, Resource Page P for ideas).

- In pairs, the children tell each other what happened at the beginning of the myth and what happened at the end of the story. Take some feedback to check recall of story.

- Display the flow chart (Resource Page E). Look at the first picture and ask, *Which part of the story does this picture tell?* Demonstrate telling the first part of the story as a narrative using the picture as a prompt.

Independent, pair or guided work

- In pairs, the children complete drawings/pictures on a whiteboard or the blank frame on Resource Page F for the remaining four boxes on the flow chart as they recall the main events in the story.

Plenary

- In pairs, the children rehearse telling of part of the story to accompany one particular box in the flow chart.

- Select pairs of children to retell parts of the story in order to retell the whole story.

- Ask the children to identify the language features in the checklist during the retelling.

Planning for Writing

Objective

We will plan our own myth

You need: Resource Pages E, G and H; OHT, OHP and pens; whiteboards; flip chart.

Whole class work

- Review the structure of a myth using the flow chart (Resource Page E) and the checklist from the previous lesson.

- Ask the children to work with their response partner to respond to questions that will reinforce the structure of a myth, for example, **What problem was there in the myth we read yesterday? How was the problem resolved? Who were the main characters?**

- Use the checklist and flow chart to model a planning frame for your own myth (see Resource Page H). During the teacher demonstration writing ensure that you:
  - explain each of your choices for the structure
  - make references to a myth the children are familiar with to reinforce the structure
  - do not complete the plan in order – it is important to know what the problem is and how it will be resolved, before planning the opening and the character details.
  - remind the children to use note form for planning, and not to write in complete sentences.
  - explain that you are going to keep the problem the same, but change the characters, setting, resolution and ending
  - tell your story so the children can see how the notes link together as a narrative.

- During the modelling of the planning, demonstrate turning some of your planning notes into a complete sentence. In pairs, the children practise doing the same with other parts of the planning notes.

Independent, pair or guided work

- Using Resource Page G or a whiteboard, the children work individually, in pairs or small groups to plan out their story. Remind them not to change the natural phenomena and to use the same traditional opening that you have. Select a pair or group to write their plan on an OHT.

- Lower attaining children can work in a group with a scribe to plan their story. They could write it independently even though they all use the same plan. Alternatively, a group story may be more appropriate.

Plenary

- Use the plan on the OHT to review the writing of notes when planning.

- Challenge the children to work with a partner to put the notes from one part of the OHT plan into a sentence.

- Use the plan on the OHT to demonstrate checking that the notes on the right-hand side of the page answer the points on the left-hand side.

- Select one or two children to tell the opening of their story from their planning frame.

The Opening

Objective

We will identify the types of words and sentences an author uses in the opening of a myth

You need: Resource Pages A, C, J, M and P; books containing myths.

Whole class work

- Read the opening of *Rainbow Bird* together (Resource Page A) and identify what the author tells the reader in the opening section of the myth.

- Read the opening again and this time ask the children to think about the words and sentences the author has used.

- Ask questions to draw out the language and sentence features, for example:
  - *Which words describe the crocodile?*
  - *What do we call words that describe?*
  - *What words does the author use at the beginning?*
  - *Why does he use them?*

- Use the children's responses to build up a checklist (see checklist 2, Resource Page P for ideas) and annotate the text to show the features identified (Resource Page C).

Independent, pair or guided work

- Using Resource Page J, the children annotate the opening of *Baira and the Vultures Who Owned Fire*, looking for the features of openings identified on the checklist and any other features they feel are important.

- Allow less able children to annotate the text used in the whole class work as this means they do not need to struggle with the reading of an unfamiliar text.

Plenary

- Use an OHT of the opening of *Baira* to annotate together (Resource Page M).

- Discuss the traditional openings. *Why are those words used instead of other traditional openings such as 'Once upon a time' or 'One day'?*

- Model some alternative openings suitable for a myth:

> Many moons ago …
>
> Long, long ago, back in the far mists of time …
>
> In far off times …

- Working in pairs, the children think of some other openings suitable for their myth.

Writing an Opening

Objective

We will write an opening for our own myth

You need: Resource Pages G and I; OHTs; tape recorder (optional).

Whole class work

- Working in pairs, ask the children to think of three features from your class checklist for the opening of a myth.

- Take feedback, then review the checklist on the flip chart from the previous lesson.

- Remind the children of the planning frame (Resource Page G) and review the elements that should be included at the beginning of a myth.

- Use Resource Page I to model writing the opening of a myth using the planning frame and checklist. Throughout the modelled writing ensure that you:
  - explain verbally the decisions you are making as a writer
  - use it as an opportunity to show the application of spelling strategies in writing, for example, using phonic knowledge to spell particular words
  - use it as an opportunity to revise letter formation or letter joining
  - refer back to the checklist and encourage the children to identify what you have used from the checklist
  - rehearse sentences aloud before committing them to paper
  - reread your work and edit
  - refer back to the planning frame
  - involve the children in contributing some ideas, for example, adjectives to describe the character.

- Following the modelled writing, pairs of children orally rehearse the opening line of their myth using their own planning frame. You may need to review some of the suggested starts from the plenary the day before.

- Take feedback from selected pairs to ensure that all have a starting point to their independent work.

Independent, pair or guided work

- Using their own planning frame, the checklist and the modelled writing, the children write the opening to their own myth.

- Select one or two pairs to write their opening on an OHT.

- Some children could word-process their openings or use a tape recorder to record it orally.

Plenary

- Use the opening on the OHT to demonstrate checking the writing against the checklist.

- In pairs, ask the children to check their partner's opening against the checklist and evaluate using a response sandwich: one good comment; one idea for improvement; another good comment.

- The children then edit and improve their openings.

The Build-up

Objective

We will find out what language features (types of words and sentences) an author uses when writing the build-up of a myth

You need: Resource Pages A, C, J, M and P; whiteboards.

Whole class work

- Read together the build-up of *Rainbow Bird* (Resource Page A).

- Spend some time over the dialogue, discussing the expression needed to suit the characters.

- Divide the class – half to be the Crocodile and half the Bird Woman. Rehearse the dialogue with the children using appropriate expression.

- Ask the children to discuss with their response partner what happens in the build-up of the myth.

- Annotate the text with the features children identify and make a checklist that may include:

> Introduce a second character (the goody)
>
> We find out a bit more about the problem

(See Resource Page C for other ideas.)

- Use questioning and discussion to build up a checklist of the language features (types of words and sentences) the author uses (see checklist 3, Resource Page P).

Independent, pair or guided work

- Using the build-up from *Baira and the Vultures Who Owned Fire* (Resource Page J), the children annotate the text with the language features identified on the checklist.

Plenary

- Go through the checklist and ask the children to give examples of the language features they found in their text. ***Did you find anything different to add to the checklist?*** (Refer to Resource Page M.)

- On whiteboards, the children draw two columns. In one they write any powerful verbs to describe how the Crocodile speaks and in the other powerful verbs to describe how the Rainbow Bird speaks.

- Take feedback and discuss what those verbs tell us about the character.

Writing the Build-up

Objective

We will write a build-up for our own myth

You need: Resource Pages H, I and P; OHTs.

Whole class work

- In pairs, ask the children to think of three things that were on the checklist for the build-up of a myth. Take feedback and check them off on the checklist.

- Refer the children back to the planning frame modelled earlier in the week (Resource Page H) and remind them of ideas for writing the build-up, for example, including the second character and adding some more information about the problem.

- Go back and read the beginning of the myth modelled in the previous lesson and orally rehearse the main points for the next part of the story.

- Use Resource Page I to model a build-up for a myth using the checklist (see checklist 3, Resource Page P for ideas) and planning frame.

- Throughout the modelled writing ensure you involve the children in contributing some ideas, for example, what the characters might say to each other.

- During the modelled writing ask the children to take on the roles of the characters to rehearse the speech before committing them to paper. The role-play should help them to select appropriate powerful verbs to follow the speech.

- Before starting independent work, ask the children (in pairs) to decide where their second character will be at the beginning of the next part of the story. They should then rehearse the opening sentence for their build-up.

Independent, pair or guided work

- Using their own planning frame, the checklist and the modelled writing, the children write their own build-up to their myth.

- Select one or two pairs to write their build-up on an OHT.

Plenary

- Use the build-up on the OHT to demonstrate checking the writing against the checklist.

- Ask the children to check their own build-up against the checklist and change and improve it.

- Ask pairs to take a character each from their build-up and role-play the dialogue between the characters. **What can we tell about the characters from the way they speak?**

(Pupil copymaster)

Rainbow Bird – opening and build-up

Long ago in the Time of Dreams when the world was being born, there lived a rough, tough Crocodile Man. He was huge and mean and scary, and he had one thing nobody else had.

Fire! Fire was his alone. Sometimes he held it with his foot. Sometimes he breathed it from his throat. Sometimes he balanced it on his head. He liked to play with Fire.

Fire was his. Alone.

When other animals begged for Fire, Crocodile Man just laughed. If they came too close he frightened them away, snarling and snapping his jaws.

"I'm boss for Fire," he growled through his teeth. "I'm boss for Fire!"

In a nearby tree lived Bird Woman. She could never get close to Fire. So she had no light in the dark, she was cold at night and she ate her fish and lizards raw.

Often she pleaded with Crocodile Man for Fire, but every time he snapped back, "Eat your food raw!"

"But what about people?" Bird Woman asked sadly. "How are they to cook their food?"

"They must eat it raw too," croaked the cross Crocodile, knocking her away with his tail. "You will not have my firesticks."

"You're so mean," sighed Bird Woman. "If I had Fire I'd give it to you." And she flew back up into the tree.

Eric Maddern

(Pupil copymaster)

Rainbow Bird – climax, resolution and ending

Time passed. From her tree Bird Woman watched Crocodile Man. And she flew about, catching her food, eating it raw, shivering with cold at night. But always watching and waiting, waiting and watching.

Then one afternoon …

Crocodile Man opened his jaws and gave the widest, longest, sleepiest, biggest yawn anyone had ever seen.

Now's my chance, thought Bird Woman. She flashed down from the tree, snatched up the firesticks and flew back into the air. And there was nothing Crocodile Man could do.

"Now I shall give Fire to the people," said Bird Woman, feeling proud, and she flew around the country putting Fire into the heart of every tree.

From that day on, people could make Fire using dry sticks and logs from a tree. And they could cook their food, keep warm at night and light their way in the dark. Then Bird Woman did a little dance and put the firesticks into her tail. She became the most beautiful Rainbow Bird.

Now Rainbow Bird flew back to Crocodile Man. "You must stay down there in the wet," she said. "I'll fly high in the dry. I'll be a bird. I'll stay on top. I'll live in the air. If you come up here you might die!"

And to this day Crocodile lives down in the swamp. His Fire has gone now, but when he growls and opens his mouth he still seems to say, "I'm boss … I'm boss!"

And Rainbow Bird? She lives in the sky and sometimes if you're lucky, you can see her still taking Fire to the trees in a blaze of feathers rainbow bright.

Eric Maddern

(Exemplar analysis)

Example of analysis of *Rainbow Bird – opening and build-up*

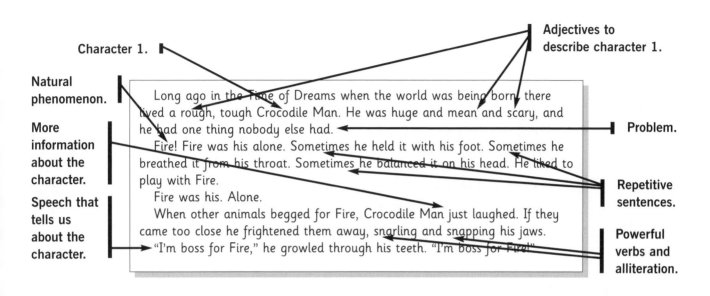

Adjectives to describe character 1.

Character 1.

Natural phenomenon.

More information about the character.

Speech that tells us about the character.

Long ago in the Time of Dreams when the world was being born, there lived a rough, tough Crocodile Man. He was huge and mean and scary, and he had one thing nobody else had.

Fire! Fire was his alone. Sometimes he held it with his foot. Sometimes he breathed it from his throat. Sometimes he balanced it on his head. He liked to play with Fire.

Fire was his. Alone.

When other animals begged for Fire, Crocodile Man just laughed. If they came too close he frightened them away, snarling and snapping his jaws. "I'm boss for Fire," he growled through his teeth. "I'm boss for Fire!"

Problem.

Repetitive sentences.

Powerful verbs and alliteration.

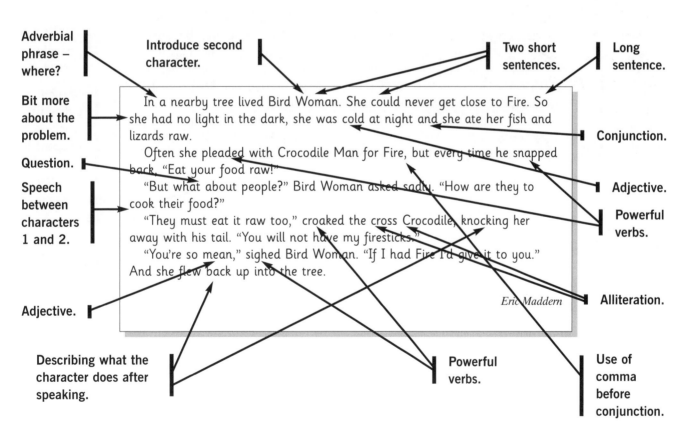

Adverbial phrase – where?

Introduce second character.

Two short sentences.

Long sentence.

Bit more about the problem.

In a nearby tree lived Bird Woman. She could never get close to Fire. So she had no light in the dark, she was cold at night and she ate her fish and lizards raw.

Conjunction.

Question.

Often she pleaded with Crocodile Man for Fire, but every time he snapped back, "Eat your food raw!"

Speech between characters 1 and 2.

"But what about people?" Bird Woman asked sadly. "How are they to cook their food?"

"They must eat it raw too," croaked the cross Crocodile, knocking her away with his tail. "You will not have my firesticks."

"You're so mean," sighed Bird Woman. "If I had Fire I'd give it to you." And she flew back up into the tree.

Eric Maddern

Adjective.

Powerful verbs.

Alliteration.

Adjective.

Describing what the character does after speaking.

Powerful verbs.

Use of comma before conjunction.

(Exemplar analysis)

Example of analysis of *Rainbow Bird – climax, resolution and ending*

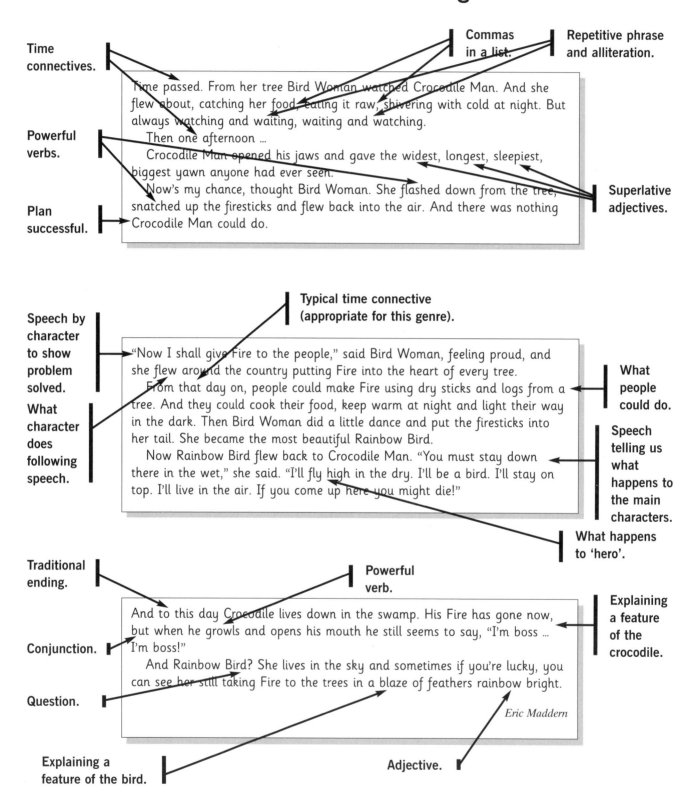

Time connectives.

Commas in a list.

Repetitive phrase and alliteration.

Time passed. From her tree Bird Woman watched Crocodile Man. And she flew about, catching her food, eating it raw, shivering with cold at night. But always watching and waiting, waiting and watching.
  Then one afternoon ...
  Crocodile Man opened his jaws and gave the widest, longest, sleepiest, biggest yawn anyone had ever seen.
  Now's my chance, thought Bird Woman. She flashed down from the tree, snatched up the firesticks and flew back into the air. And there was nothing Crocodile Man could do.

Powerful verbs.

Plan successful.

Superlative adjectives.

Speech by character to show problem solved.

What character does following speech.

Typical time connective (appropriate for this genre).

"Now I shall give Fire to the people," said Bird Woman, feeling proud, and she flew around the country putting Fire into the heart of every tree.
  From that day on, people could make Fire using dry sticks and logs from a tree. And they could cook their food, keep warm at night and light their way in the dark. Then Bird Woman did a little dance and put the firesticks into her tail. She became the most beautiful Rainbow Bird.
  Now Rainbow Bird flew back to Crocodile Man. "You must stay down there in the wet," she said. "I'll fly high in the dry. I'll be a bird. I'll stay on top. I'll live in the air. If you come up here you might die!"

What people could do.

Speech telling us what happens to the main characters.

What happens to 'hero'.

Traditional ending.

Powerful verb.

And to this day Crocodile lives down in the swamp. His Fire has gone now, but when he growls and opens his mouth he still seems to say, "I'm boss ... I'm boss!"
  And Rainbow Bird? She lives in the sky and sometimes if you're lucky, you can see her still taking Fire to the trees in a blaze of feathers rainbow bright.

Eric Maddern

Conjunction.

Question.

Explaining a feature of the crocodile.

Explaining a feature of the bird.

Adjective.

(Pupil copymaster)

Flow chart

(Pupil copymaster)

Blank flow chart

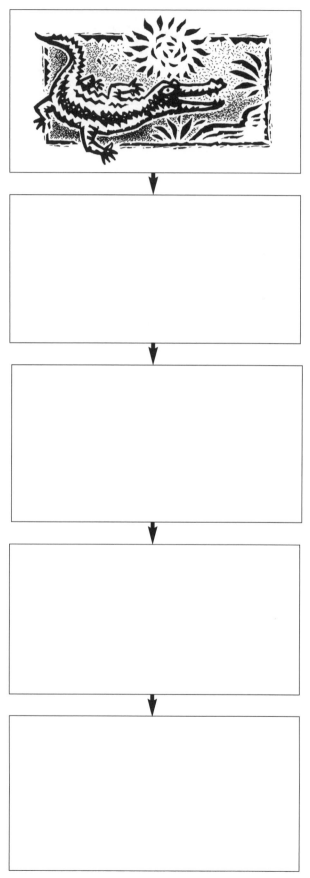

Planning frame

Traditional opening	
Natural phenomena	
Setting	
Characters	
What are the characters like?	
What is the problem?	
Who is going to steal the fire?	
What is the plan?	
How will we know it is resolved (sorted out)?	
Traditional ending	

(Pupil copymaster)

Modelled planning frame

Traditional opening	Long, long ago.
Natural phenomena	Fire.
Setting	Jungle.
Characters	Snake and monkey.
What are the characters like?	Snake – sneaky, slithery and selfish. Flicks fireball from tail to head. Monkey – quick and clever.
What is the problem?	Snake has got fire and won't let anyone else have it. Everyone else is cold and has no light or fire for cooking.
Who is going to steal the fire?	Monkey.
What is the plan?	Steal it from snake when flicking it.
How will we know it is resolved (sorted out)?	Monkey swings through trees, putting fire into them.
Traditional ending	Snake stays on jungle floor away from monkey. Monkey still clever at taking things from people.

(Exemplar material)

Modelled writing

Opening
Long, long ago, when the earth was cold and dark, there lived a slithery, sneaky snake. He was mean and selfish and he had one thing nobody else had. He had fire. Sometimes he would roll it out on his long, forked tongue. Sometimes he would flick it from his head to his tail. Sometimes he would roll it on the dry, dusty ground. When the other animals asked him for fire, he would hiss, "It's mine, steal it if you can."

Build up
High up in the trees swung a quick and clever monkey. He knew that fire should be for everyone to share. Everyday he would beg for fire from the snake, but every time the selfish snake would hiss, "It's mine, steal it if you can."

"But we need heat and light," pleaded the monkey.

"It must stay cold and dark," snarled the selfish snake and slithered back to his rock to play with the fireballs.

"You will *not* keep it to yourself," shouted the monkey and he scampered up to the top of the nearest tree to think of a plan.

Climax
A few weeks passed. The monkey had thought of a plan. He watched and waited and waited and watched until one afternoon he saw the snake flicking fire between his head and tail.

"You must be the cleverest snake in the jungle. Please show me how you flick fire from your head to your tail," said the monkey.

Now's my chance thought the monkey. Quick as a flash, he grabbed the ball of fire as it flew through the air. He held it close to his chest and hurtled back up to the top of the trees, far away from the snake.

Resolution
"Now you shall all have fire," he sung as he flew through the jungle putting fire into the heart of every tree.

From that day on, people could make fire, using wood from trees. Everyone would cook their food, keep warm and light their way in the dark.

As for the snake, he decided to stay away from the monkeys in case they tricked him again.

Ending
And to this day the snake lives down on the dark, damp jungle floor, hardly ever climbing the trees, but he still hisses, "It's mine" every time anyone goes near him.

And the monkey? He still swings from tree to tree in the jungle. If you've ever been near a monkey you'll know that they are quick and clever at stealing things from anyone not paying close attention.

Classworks Literacy Year 3 © Carolyn Bray, Nelson Thornes Ltd 2003

Baira and the Vultures Who Owned Fire – opening and build-up

There was a time, long, long ago, when humans did not have fire. Only one animal had fire. That was the vulture and it kept it under its wings. Can you imagine that? Human beings had to eat food raw, or hang it up to dry in the sun. The humans wanted fire as well. But they could not think of a way to get it. They knew that vultures were proud to be the owners of fire. They knew vultures had quick wings and sharp claws. They knew that vultures were very crafty.

But at that time, in a tribe called the Parintintin, there was a young Indian and his name was Baira. He was barely a man, but he was very brave and very clever. He said that as the earth, the water and the sunshine had no owner then fire should be for everyone too.

So he gathered all the people of his tribe together. Then he told them his plan to steal fire from the vultures.

Retold by Sean Taylor

Baira and the Vultures Who Owned Fire – climax

The next day, first thing in the morning, Baira went into the forest and covered himself in dead leaves and maggots. He lay down on the ground and there he stayed. Imagine that, lying there with maggots dancing all over you! But there he stayed, half hidden on the floor of the rainforest.

Well, after a bit he heard this ZUM … ZUM … ZUM. It was a blue fly. The blue fly buzzed and buzzed up above Baira. Then it flew off. And do you know where it went? Well, I'll tell you. It went to tell the vulture that there was a dead man lying on the forest floor.

Now the vulture did not waste any time, did he?

"A dead man!" he squawked. "Yeah, let's go!"

So he called his wife, his son, his grandmother, his wife's grandfather, his brother-in-law, his cousin, his cousin's great-grandmother and his cousin's great-grandmother's nephew and they all flew through the forest to eat the dead man lying on the forest floor.

When they got there, the vulture lifted up its wing and set fire to a stick so that they could begin to cook Baira. A flame began to flicker brightly. Baira opened one eye but didn't move. He waited for exactly the right moment. He waited until the stick was burning strongly. Then he sprang up, snatched it and started to run for his village.

Well! That young man, he ran like the wind! He dodged between small trees! He leapt over pools of water! He ducked under vines! The vultures came flapping furiously after him. They squawked. They screeched. And they scratched at the air with their sharp claws.

Baira tried to hide in a tree, but the vultures found him. So he ran through thick forest where the vultures could not follow.

At last he found himself at the edge of the wide river, and to get back to his village he had to cross it. How was he going to swim, holding a burning stick? The river was too wide. So he called the green river-snake. He shouted:

"River-snake! Take the burning stick to the other side of the river and give fire to my tribe."

Well, the river-snake swam with the burning stick coiled in her tail. She headed for the middle of the river, but her scales were burning – turning brown. And that's why river-snakes are brown to this day.

"Someone help!" she called. "My scales are burning! I can't hold the fire any longer!"

So Baira called the prawn.

"Prawn! Take the burning stick to the other side of the river and give fire to my tribe."

So the prawn swam balancing the burning stick on his whiskers. He nearly got to the middle of the river, but his tail was burning – turning pink. And that is why prawns are pink to this day.

"Help! Help!" he called. "My tail is burning! I can't hold the fire any longer!"

So Baira called the cururu-frog.

"Cururu-frog! Take the burning stick to the other side of the river and give fire to my tribe."

So the cururu-frog swam with the burning stick in its mouth. The fire was burning its face but it was nearly across the river, so it swam on. The people from Baira's tribe splashed into the water, took the burning stick, and held it up in the air.

Retold by Sean Taylor

Baira and the Vultures Who Owned Fire – resolution and ending

Well! There was a party that night all right. The Parintintins celebrated for a whole week with songs and dances around a huge fire. And ever since that time, humans have had fire to cook their food and light their way in the night. Baira grew up to be the great hero of his tribe.

And what about the cururu-frog? Well, because it was the one that finally got fire to the other side of the river, it became a magic animal. It became the only animal that can eat fire-flies without burning its mouth. And you know, to this day, it is still the only one that can.

Retold by Sean Taylor

(Exemplar analysis)

Example of analysis of *Baira – opening and build-up*

Traditional opening.

Introduce natural phenomenon.

Question for reader.

Repetitive sentences.

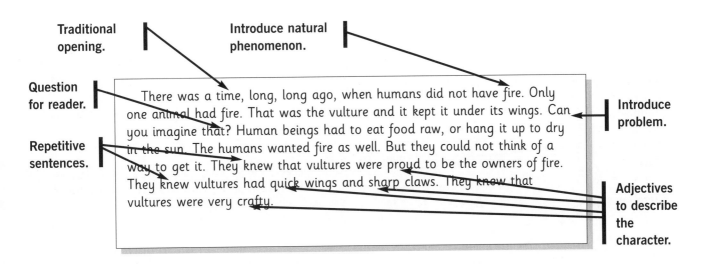

There was a time, long, long ago, when humans did not have fire. Only one animal had fire. That was the vulture and it kept it under its wings. Can you imagine that? Human beings had to eat food raw, or hang it up to dry in the sun. The humans wanted fire as well. But they could not think of a way to get it. They knew that vultures were proud to be the owners of fire. They knew vultures had quick wings and sharp claws. They knew that vultures were very crafty.

Introduce problem.

Adjectives to describe the character.

Adverbial phrase – when.

Introduce character 2.

Setting.

Use of comma before conjunction.

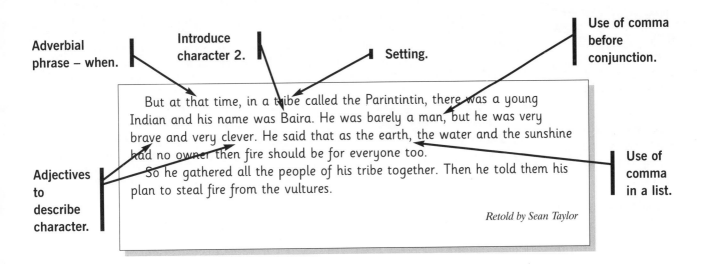

But at that time, in a tribe called the Parintintin, there was a young Indian and his name was Baira. He was barely a man, but he was very brave and very clever. He said that as the earth, the water and the sunshine had no owner then fire should be for everyone too.
So he gathered all the people of his tribe together. Then he told them his plan to steal fire from the vultures.

Retold by Sean Taylor

Adjectives to describe character.

Use of comma in a list.

(Exemplar analysis)

Example of analysis of *Baira – climax*

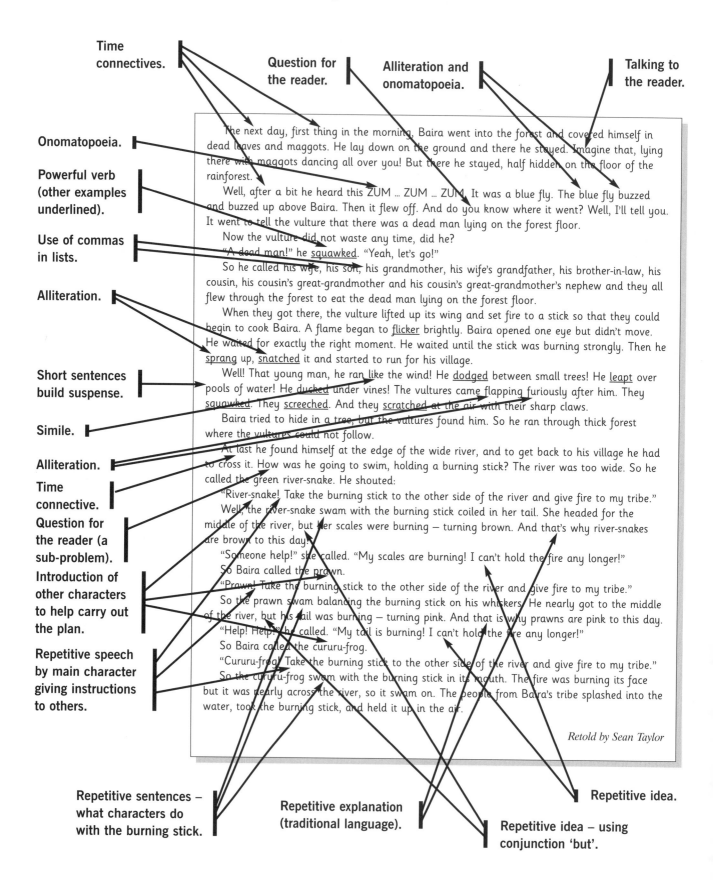

Time connectives.

Question for the reader.

Alliteration and onomatopoeia.

Talking to the reader.

Onomatopoeia.

Powerful verb (other examples underlined).

Use of commas in lists.

Alliteration.

Short sentences build suspense.

Simile.

Alliteration.

Time connective.

Question for the reader (a sub-problem).

Introduction of other characters to help carry out the plan.

Repetitive speech by main character giving instructions to others.

The next day, first thing in the morning, Baira went into the forest and covered himself in dead leaves and maggots. He lay down on the ground and there he stayed. Imagine that, lying there with maggots dancing all over you! But there he stayed, half hidden on the floor of the rainforest.

Well, after a bit he heard this ZUM … ZUM … ZUM. It was a blue fly. The blue fly buzzed and buzzed up above Baira. Then it flew off. And do you know where it went? Well, I'll tell you. It went to tell the vulture that there was a dead man lying on the forest floor.

Now the vulture did not waste any time, did he?

"A dead man!" he squawked. "Yeah, let's go!"

So he called his wife, his son, his grandmother, his wife's grandfather, his brother-in-law, his cousin, his cousin's great-grandmother and his cousin's great-grandmother's nephew and they all flew through the forest to eat the dead man lying on the forest floor.

When they got there, the vulture lifted up its wing and set fire to a stick so that they could begin to cook Baira. A flame began to flicker brightly. Baira opened one eye but didn't move. He waited for exactly the right moment. He waited until the stick was burning strongly. Then he sprang up, snatched it and started to run for his village.

Well! That young man, he ran like the wind! He dodged between small trees! He leapt over pools of water! He ducked under vines! The vultures came flapping furiously after him. They squawked. They screeched. And they scratched at the air with their sharp claws.

Baira tried to hide in a tree, but the vultures found him. So he ran through thick forest where the vultures could not follow.

At last he found himself at the edge of the wide river, and to get back to his village he had to cross it. How was he going to swim, holding a burning stick? The river was too wide. So he called the green river-snake. He shouted:

"River-snake! Take the burning stick to the other side of the river and give fire to my tribe."

Well, the river-snake swam with the burning stick coiled in her tail. She headed for the middle of the river, but her scales were burning – turning brown. And that's why river-snakes are brown to this day.

"Someone help!" she called. "My scales are burning! I can't hold the fire any longer!"

So Baira called the prawn.

"Prawn! Take the burning stick to the other side of the river and give fire to my tribe."

So the prawn swam balancing the burning stick on his whiskers. He nearly got to the middle of the river, but his tail was burning – turning pink. And that is why prawns are pink to this day.

"Help! Help!" he called. "My tail is burning! I can't hold the fire any longer!"

So Baira called the cururu-frog.

"Cururu-frog! Take the burning stick to the other side of the river and give fire to my tribe."

So the cururu-frog swam with the burning stick in its mouth. The fire was burning its face but it was nearly across the river, so it swam on. The people from Baira's tribe splashed into the water, took the burning stick, and held it up in the air.

Retold by Sean Taylor

Repetitive sentences – what characters do with the burning stick.

Repetitive explanation (traditional language).

Repetitive idea – using conjunction 'but'.

Repetitive idea.

(Exemplar analysis)

Example of analysis of *Baira – resolution and ending*

What happens to 'hero'.

Typical time connective.

What people could do now.

> Well! There was a party that night all right. The Parintintins celebrated for a whole week with songs and dances around a huge fire. And ever since that time, humans have had fire to cook their food and light their way in the night. Baira grew up to be the great hero of his tribe.

Question for the reader.

Explaining a feature of the cururu-frog.

> And what about the cururu-frog? Well, because it was the one that finally got fire to the other side of the river, it became a magic animal. It became the only animal that can eat fire-flies without burning its mouth. And you know, to this day, it is still the only one that can.
>
> *Retold by Sean Taylor*

Traditional ending phrase.

(Exemplar material)

Checklists for myths

Example of a checklist for a myth

- Include a 'timeless' opening

- Describe natural phenomena

- Describe setting

- Include a problem

- Describe characters – goody and baddy

- Include a plan to solve the problem

- Use a traditional ending, for example, 'from that day on' or 'to this day'

Example of a checklist for the opening

- Include a traditional opening

- Use adjectives to describe the character

- Describe the problem

- Describe the natural phenomena

- Use repetitive sentences

- Use powerful verbs

- Use alliteration

- Include speech that tells us about the character

Example of a checklist for the build-up

- Introduce a second character (the goody)

- We find out a bit more about the problem

- Include a speech between the two characters

- Use alliteration

- Use short sentences

- Use long sentences which use conjunctions: 'and', 'but'

- Include commas being used in long sentences

- Use powerful verbs and interesting adjectives

- Use an adverbial phrase to tell us 'where' the action takes place

- Describe what the characters do after speaking

Continued ...

Checklists for myths (continued)

Example of a checklist for the climax

- Use time connectives
- Explain what the character is doing to carry out the plan
- Use short repetitive and alliterative phrases
- Use superlative adjectives
- Use powerful verbs

The second text also uses:

- Onomatopoeia
- Simile
- Short sentences to build suspense
- Introduction of other characters to help carry out the plan
- Question or statement for the reader

Example of a checklist for the resolution

- Include speech to show problem is solved
- Follow speech by saying what the character is doing
- Use a time connective particular to the genre, for example, 'from that day on…'
- Include a sentence telling us what humans could do now
- Describe what happens to the main character

Example of a checklist for the ending

- Use a traditional ending, for example, 'and to this day…'
- Use the present tense
- Answer questions explaining why characters have a particular feature
- Include a sentence with a conjunction
- Use interesting adjectives and powerful verbs

(Marking ladder)

Name: _____

Pupil	Objective	Teacher
	My myth includes a beginning, a build-up, a climax, a resolution and an ending.	
	I explained a natural phenomena.	
	I used a traditional opening and ending.	
	I used adjectives and powerful verbs to help describe characters.	
	I used alliteration.	
	I used repetitive sentences.	
	I included a speech between the main characters.	
	I used time connectives.	
	I included an adverbial phrase.	
	I included a sentence with 'but' in it.	
	I included a question.	
	What could I do to improve my myth next time?	

Instruction Texts

Outcome

A set of instructions for cleaning your teeth

Objectives

Sentence

10 to understand the differences between verbs in the 1st, 2nd and 3rd person through relating to different types of text, e.g. 1st person for diaries, personal letters, 2nd person for instructions, directions, 3rd person for narrative, recounts.

12 to identify the different purposes of instructional texts, e.g. recipes, route-finders, timetables, instructions, plans, rules.

13 to discuss the merits and limitations of particular instructional texts, including IT and other media texts, and to compare these with others, where appropriate, to give an overall evaluation.

Text

14 [be taught] how written instructions are organised, e.g. lists, numbered points, diagrams with arrows, bullet points, keys.

15 to read and follow simple instructions.

16 to write instructions, e.g. rules for playing games, recipes, using a range of organisational devices, e.g. lists, dashes, commas for lists in sentences, while recognising the importance of correct sequence; use writing frames as appropriate for support.

Planning frame

- Read examples of instructions, noting purpose and features.
- Write own instructions and diagrams for different purposes.

Notes

- This unit can be linked with the QCA Science units 'Teeth and Eating' or 'Helping Plants Grow Well'.
- To extend this unit, give the children the opportunity to write instructions that link with other curricular areas, for example, Design and Technology.
- The writing of instructions, particularly text layout, is suited to the use of ICT. If possible, the writing elements of this unit should be taught in an ICT suite.

How you could plan this unit

Day 1	Day 2	Day 3	Day 4	Day 5
Speaking and listening	Reading	Reading	Reading and writing	Reading and writing List of equipment. Spelling focus – compound words
Organising Instructions	*Thinking about Purpose*	*Language Features*	*Title and Tantaliser*	

Day 6	Day 7	Day 8	Day 9	Day 10
Reading and writing Sentence-level work on verbs, for example, *Grammar for Writing* Unit 14	Reading and writing Instructions and diagrams	Reading and writing Instructions and diagrams	Reading and writing Extra information or tip	Speaking and listening Evaluate instructions and mark using marking ladder

Organising Instructions

Objective

We will listen to and follow instructions and think about how the way they are organised helps us to follow them

You need: Resource Page A; kettle, teapot, teabag, teacup and saucer, milk, spoon, sugar; scrap paper; whiteboards and pens; flip chart.

Whole class work

- After introducing the objectives, give the children some instructions to follow:
  - *Stand up, put your chairs in and come and sit on the carpet.*
  - *Sit next to your response partner.*
  - *Jack, give out the whiteboards and pens one between two.*

  Ask the children what you were doing and why you were doing it.

- With their response partners, the children think of some other instructions they have been given today and maybe some instructions they have given themselves.

- Take feedback, making the point that we listen, give and follow instructions many times during a day.

- Tell the children that they are going to work with their response partner to give you instructions to make a cup of tea.

- Demonstrate the first instruction yourself and carry it out. Then ask the children to discuss with their response partner and suggest the next instruction. The children could write some of their instructions on whiteboards and some could be given orally.

- A teaching assistant (or an able child) scribes the instructions on the flip chart. When the instructions are complete, discuss with the children the importance of giving them in the correct order.

- Discuss the importance of having a 'You will need ...' list (this may come up earlier in the session).

Independent, pair or guided work

- Using Resource Page A on making a paper aeroplane, children cut up the page to sequence the instructions correctly, then follow them to make the aeroplane using scrap paper.

- *What clues helped you to sequence the instructions correctly? How easy were the instructions to follow?*

Plenary

- Discuss and list the features of the text organisation that made it easy to follow:

numbering
diagrams
the title
small amounts of writing

- Evaluate how easy the instructions were to follow. *How would you change them to make them easier to follow?*

Thinking about Purpose

Objective

We will identify the purpose and organisation of an instruction text

You need: Resource Pages B (OHT or A3 copy), C, D and G (all on OHT); bulb, pot and compost.

Whole class work

- Read the title of Resource Page B – *Planting a bulb*. Ask the children to predict what the purpose of the instructions might be.

- Read the text together.

- *What made the instructions easy to follow?* Answer: the organisation and layout of the text. Use the feedback and discussion to annotate the text with the features identified by the children (see Resource Page C) and to make a checklist of text structure (see checklist 1, Resource Page G for ideas).

Independent, pair or guided work

- The children identify and annotate the features of text structures and layout on the checklist in another instructional text (Resource Page D).

- In pairs, the children discuss the purpose for the instructions.

Plenary

- The children give examples of the features they have found from the checklist on the previous text.

- *Were there any other features not on the original checklist?*

- Remind the children how the organisation of the text helps the reader to follow instructions. *Which set of instructions did you think were better? Why?*

Language Features

Objective

We will identify the language features (types of words and sentences) used in instructions

You need: Resource Pages B, D (on OHT) and G.

Whole class work

- With their response partners, ask the children to recall as many features from the last lesson's checklist as they can.

- Show the children the instructions for planting a bulb (Resource Page B) with the annotations from the previous lesson. Review today's objective and remind the children to think about the types of words and sentences the writer is using as you read the text together.

- Use feedback and discussion to annotate the text with the features identified and make a checklist (see checklist 2, Resource Page G for ideas).

Independent, pair or guided work

- The children identify the language features from the checklist and annotate Resource Page D, *A tasty snack*.

Plenary

- The children give examples of the features they found that are on the checklist. *Is there anything else to add to the checklist?* This text includes:

> extra information in brackets
>
> capital letters for an important word
>
> an exclamation mark
>
> a capital letter for a special name
>
> a time connective
>
> a question for the reader

- Discuss what words could be used on the snack instructions, in place of the numbers.

- Put a copy of the instructions on an OHT and insert time connectives suggested by the children, for example:

> first   next   after   then

- Read the text together with the time connectives, rather than the numbers. *Which makes a better set of instructions? Why?*

Title and Tantaliser

Objective

We will use the correct text and language features to write our own instructions

You need: Resource Pages B, D, F and G; word processors (one per pair or small group).

Whole class work	<ul><li>Review the previous lessons and checklists by asking the children:<ul><li>*What is the purpose of instructional writing?*</li><li>*What are some of the organisational features of instruction writing?*</li><li>*What are some of the words and sentences writers use when writing instructions?*</li></ul></li><li>Refer back to the instructions for planting a bulb (Resource Page B) and remind the children that we have a heading first and an introduction to persuade you to follow the instructions. The children reread the introductions of *Planting a bulb* and *A tasty snack* (Resource Page D) to remind them of the type of language used.</li><li>Model writing the title and the introduction (tantaliser) for a set of instructions for having a bath. You should use a word-processor for this. During the modelled writing ensure that you:<ul><li>explain all your decisions</li><li>rehearse your ideas and sentences orally before writing them down</li><li>reread your work and edit if necessary</li><li>take the opportunity to talk about spelling strategies when 'stuck' on a word</li><li>refer to the checklist</li><li>ask the children to indicate when they think you've used something on the checklist.</li></ul></li><li>Encourage the children to think about how they will write instructions for cleaning their teeth.</li><li>Discuss layout of text including font size and style, use of bold and italic options.</li><li>In pairs, the children think of the heading for their instructions. Ask them to discuss ideas for what they will say in the introduction to persuade people to follow their instructions to clean their teeth. Take feedback to ensure that the children are prepared for working independently.</li></ul>
Independent, pair or guided work	<ul><li>Using word processors, the children write their own heading and introduction for cleaning teeth using the checklists (Resource Page G) and the modelled writing (Resource Page F) as support.</li></ul>
Plenary	<ul><li>Discuss and take feedback on decisions the children took for their heading: words, font size and style.</li><li>*What is the purpose of the introduction?*</li><li>Through reading some of the introductions discuss whether they would persuade you to carry on reading the instructions.</li></ul>

(Pupil copymaster)

Making a paper aeroplane

4

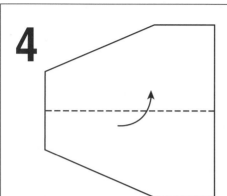

Flip over and fold in half along the centre line.

1

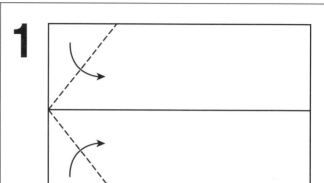

Take a rectangular sheet of paper and fold two corners into the middle.

5

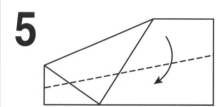

Fold the wings downwards.

3

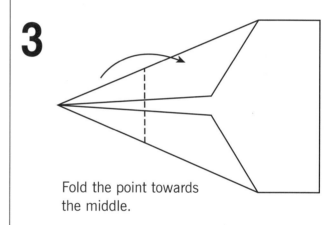

Fold the point towards the middle.

2

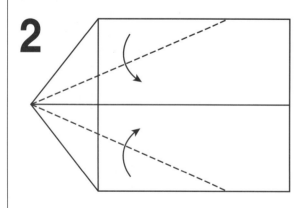

Fold into the middle again.

6

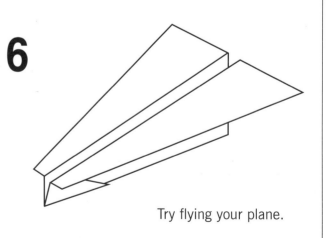

Try flying your plane.

Classworks Literacy Year 3 © Carolyn Bray, Nelson Thornes Ltd 2003

(Pupil copymaster)

Planting a bulb

Plant a hyacinth bulb in November to get a beautiful bloom in early spring.

You will need:
- *a hyacinth bulb*
- *compost*
- *a small pot with a drainage hole*
- *a label*
- *water*
- *a bowl for mixing*
- *gloves*

How to plant your bulb

- Put some compost in a bowl.
  Mix in water until the compost is moist but not soggy.

- Fill the pot with moistened compost until it is two-thirds full.

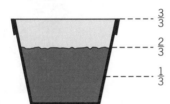

- Gently press the compost down.

- Put the bulb carefully on to the compost.

- Add more compost, pressing it firmly with your fingertips.

- Fasten your label to the pot.

- Put the bulb in a cool, dark place while the roots develop.

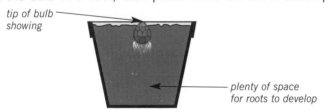

tip of bulb showing

plenty of space for roots to develop

- Check your bulb every week, making sure the compost is kept moist.

- In January, bring your bulb into a warm, light room.
  Watch the flower develop and bloom.

SAFETY NOTE
Most bulbs are poisonous and can cause allergic reactions.
***Always* wear safety gloves when handling bulbs and *always* wash your hands afterwards.**

(Exemplar analysis)

Example of analysis of *Planting a bulb*

Introductory statement ('tantaliser') to persuade you to follow the instructions.

Bold text shows subheading.

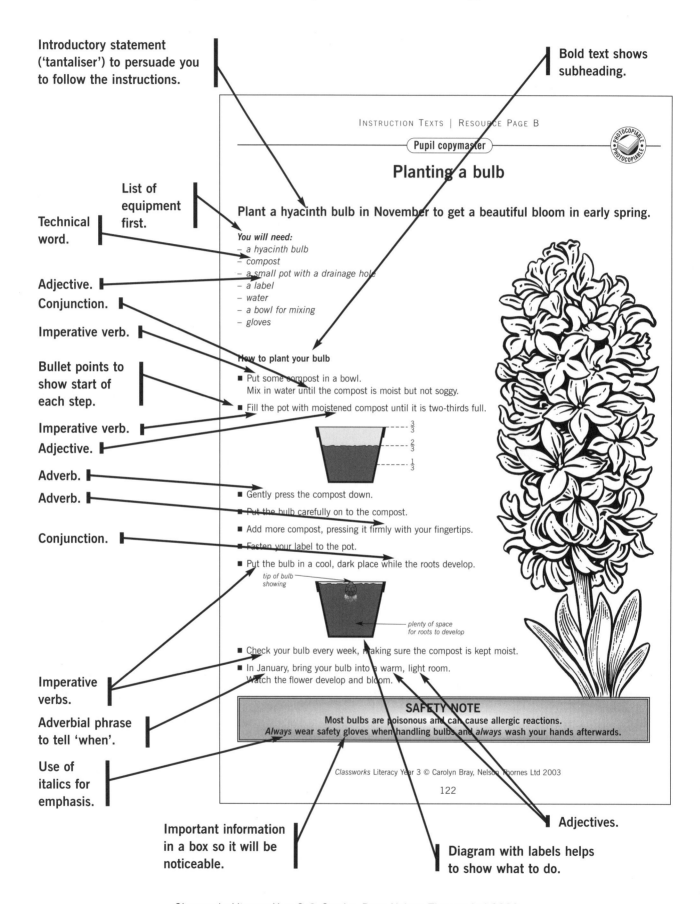

INSTRUCTION TEXTS | RESOURCE PAGE B

(Pupil copymaster)

Planting a bulb

Plant a hyacinth bulb in November to get a beautiful bloom in early spring.

You will need:
– *a hyacinth bulb*
– *compost*
– *a small pot with a drainage hole*
– *a label*
– *water*
– *a bowl for mixing*
– *gloves*

How to plant your bulb

■ Put some compost in a bowl.
Mix in water until the compost is moist but not soggy.

■ Fill the pot with moistened compost until it is two-thirds full.

$\frac{3}{3}$
$\frac{2}{3}$
$\frac{1}{3}$

■ Gently press the compost down.

■ Put the bulb carefully on to the compost.

■ Add more compost, pressing it firmly with your fingertips.

■ Fasten your label to the pot.

■ Put the bulb in a cool, dark place while the roots develop.

tip of bulb showing

plenty of space for roots to develop

■ Check your bulb every week, making sure the compost is kept moist.

■ In January, bring your bulb into a warm, light room.
Watch the flower develop and bloom.

SAFETY NOTE
Most bulbs are poisonous and can cause allergic reactions.
Always wear safety gloves when handling bulbs and *always* wash your hands afterwards.

Classworks Literacy Year 3 © Carolyn Bray, Nelson Thornes Ltd 2003

122

List of equipment first.

Technical word.

Adjective.

Conjunction.

Imperative verb.

Bullet points to show start of each step.

Imperative verb.

Adjective.

Adverb.

Adverb.

Conjunction.

Imperative verbs.

Adverbial phrase to tell 'when'.

Use of italics for emphasis.

Important information in a box so it will be noticeable.

Diagram with labels helps to show what to do.

Adjectives.

(Pupil copymaster)

A tasty snack

CHEESE ON TOAST

Sometimes it is helpful to be able to prepare food for yourself – perhaps if your parents are busy. This is a simple recipe which will need only a little help from an adult.

Ingredients

1 slice of bread – thick enough to toast
50g cheese – use a hard variety
a little butter
extras – Marmite or sauce or chutney
garnish – slices of tomato or parsley

Equipment

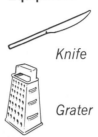

Knife

Grater

What to do

1 Switch on or light the grill. Toast the bread on ONE side only.

2 Grate the cheese. (Mind your fingers!)

3 Spread the butter on the untoasted side of the bread. Add a little Marmite, sauce or chutney, if you like.

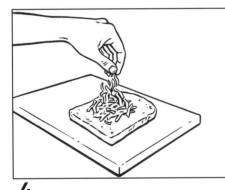

4 Pile the grated cheese on top. Make sure you cover all the bread. Press down lightly.

5 Replace under the grill and toast.

6 When golden arrange on a plate. Decorate with a sprig of parsley or slices of tomato. Your snack is ready to serve.

WARNING:
Take care when lighting the grill and handling the hot grill pan. This is when adults can be really helpful!
Have you remembered to switch off the grill?

Classworks Literacy Year 3 © Carolyn Bray, Nelson Thornes Ltd 2003

Exemplar analysis

Example of analysis of *A tasty snack*

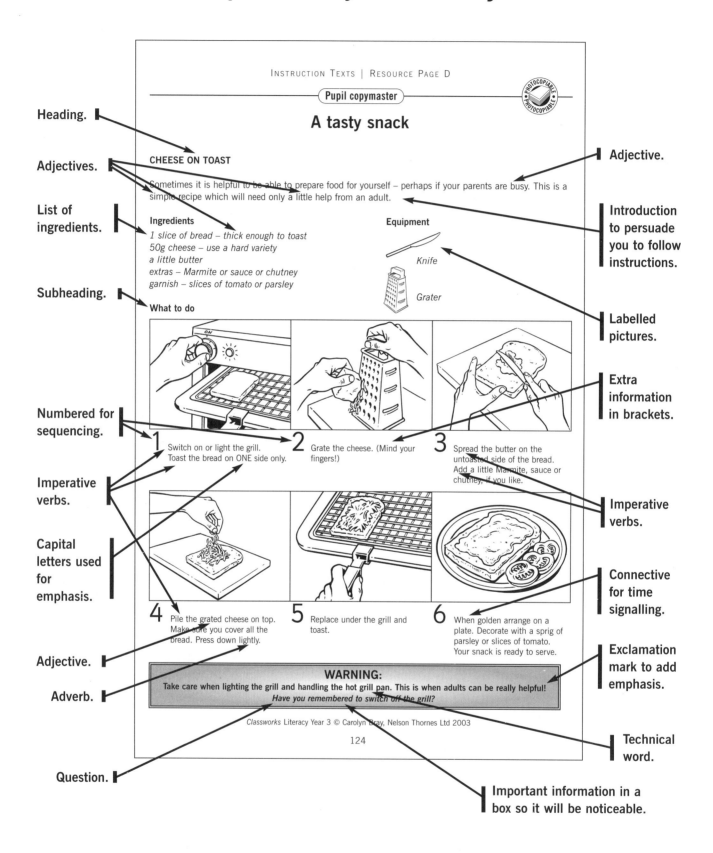

Heading.

Adjectives.

List of ingredients.

Subheading.

Numbered for sequencing.

Imperative verbs.

Capital letters used for emphasis.

Adjective.

Adverb.

Question.

Adjective.

Introduction to persuade you to follow instructions.

Labelled pictures.

Extra information in brackets.

Imperative verbs.

Connective for time signalling.

Exclamation mark to add emphasis.

Technical word.

Important information in a box so it will be noticeable.

INSTRUCTION TEXTS | RESOURCE PAGE D

Pupil copymaster

A tasty snack

CHEESE ON TOAST

Sometimes it is helpful to be able to prepare food for yourself – perhaps if your parents are busy. This is a simple recipe which will need only a little help from an adult.

Ingredients
1 slice of bread – thick enough to toast
50g cheese – use a hard variety
a little butter
extras – Marmite or sauce or chutney
garnish – slices of tomato or parsley

Equipment

Knife

Grater

What to do

1 Switch on or light the grill. Toast the bread on ONE side only.

2 Grate the cheese. (Mind your fingers!)

3 Spread the butter on the untoasted side of the bread. Add a little Marmite, sauce or chutney, if you like.

4 Pile the grated cheese on top. Make sure you cover all the bread. Press down lightly.

5 Replace under the grill and toast.

6 When golden arrange on a plate. Decorate with a sprig of parsley or slices of tomato. Your snack is ready to serve.

WARNING:
Take care when lighting the grill and handling the hot grill pan. This is when adults can be really helpful!
Have you remembered to switch off the grill?

Classworks Literacy Year 3 © Carolyn Bray, Nelson Thornes Ltd 2003

124

Classworks Literacy Year 3 © Carolyn Bray, Nelson Thornes Ltd 2003

114

Modelled writing

Bathtime

Do you want to smell as fresh as a daisy?
Do you want your skin to gleam with cleanliness?

Then follow these simple instructions and get the most out of your bathtime.

You will need:

SOAP   SPONGE   TOWEL   RUBBER DUCK   SHAMPOO (optional)
FLANNEL   BUBBLEBATH

1 Turn hot and cold taps on and fill bath with water. Add a few drops of bubblebath.

2 After undressing, check the temperature of the water before carefully climbing in. (Take care not to slip.)

3 Rub soap onto sponge or flannel and scrub body. Concentrate on neck, knees and feet (these often gather most dirt).

4 Rinse soap from body using flannel or sponge. (You may wish to wash your hair at this point.)

5 Place rubber duck and any other toys into the water and play for 5-10 minutes (without splashing).

6 Finally, remove all objects from the bath, pull out the plug and climb out. Wrap wet body in towel.

TIP: If soap or shampoo comes in contact with eyes, rinse them thoroughly with cold water.

Classworks Literacy Year 3 © Carolyn Bray, Nelson Thornes Ltd 2003

(**Exemplar material**)

Checklists for instruction texts

Example of a checklist for instruction layout

- Use a heading

- Use subheadings

- List the things you need first

- Use diagrams with labels

- Include bullet points

- Use short sentences so they are easy to follow

- Write in columns down the page

- Include a short introduction to persuade the reader to follow the instructions

- Put safety notes in a box so they are clear

- Use bold print and italic print

Example of a checklist for instruction language

- Use verbs at the beginning of sentences

- Use verbs in the imperative form ('bossy' verbs)

- Include special or technical words, for example, 'compost', 'moist', 'allergic'

- Use adverbs – to tell the reader how to do something

- Use conjunctions to join ideas together, for example, 'while', 'until'

- Use adjectives to describe more precisely, for example, 'small', 'cool', 'dark'

- Use commas between adjectives

- Use commas to help the sentence make sense

- Include an adverbial phrase telling you when

- Use capital letters for the beginning of a sentence and for months of the year

- Use the present tense

Marking ladder

Name: _____

Pupil	Objective	Teacher
	My set of instructions includes a heading, an introduction, a list of equipment, step-by-step instructions and a note or tip at the end.	
	I used bullet points, numbers or connectives to make the order clear.	
	I used diagrams to make the instructions easy to follow.	
	I used imperative or 'bossy' verbs to start instructions.	
	I made good use of adjectives, adverbs and special or technical words to be precise.	
	I used conjunctions to join two ideas together.	
	I used a comma to separate ideas.	
	I made good use of different fonts and styles, including bold, italic and capitals.	
	I used capital letters at the beginning of sentences and for special names.	
	I have asked someone to try out my instructions to see if they are easy to follow.	
	What could I do to improve my instruction writing next time?	

Classworks Literacy Year 3 © Carolyn Bray, Nelson Thornes Ltd 2003

Reviewing Books by the Same Author

Outcome

A book review

Objectives

Sentence

2 to identify pronouns and understand their functions in sentences through: distinguishing personal pronouns and possessive pronouns; distinguishing the 1st, 2nd, 3rd person forms of pronouns; investigating the contexts and purposes for using pronouns in different persons.

5 [be taught] how sentences can be joined in more complex ways through using a widening range of conjunctions in addition to 'and' and 'then'.

Text

1 to retell main points of story in sequence; to compare different stories; to evaluate stories and justify their preferences.

8 to compare and contrast works by the same author, e.g. different stories, sequels using same characters in new settings, stories sharing similar themes.

9 to be aware of authors and to discuss preferences and reasons for these.

14 to write book reviews for a specified audience, based on evaluations of plot, characters and language.

Planning frame

- Read and analyse a selection of book reviews.
- Write a review of books by a particular author.

Notes

- For this unit the children must have read books by the same author. For it to be successful, they should be familiar with *The Diary of a Killer Cat* and other books by Anne Fine, for example, *Notso Hotso, Design a Pram, Scaredy Cat*.
- This unit could be extended by making a class book of book reviews for a specific audience, such as another class or the school newspaper.

How you could plan this unit

Day 1	Day 2	Day 3	Day 4	Day 5
Reading	Reading and writing	Writing Sentence-level work, focusing on words to signal time sequences, for example, *Grammar for Writing* Unit 18	Reading and writing Children write summary of the main plot events and character sketches	Writing Sentence-level work using 'because' as a conjunction
Features of a Review	*Writing an Introduction*			

Day 6	Day 7	Day 8
Reading and writing	Reading and writing The children write recommendations for others to read	Writing Write complete book review and evaluate with marking ladder
Justifying Your Opinion		

Features of a Review

Objective

We will identify what should be included in a book review

You need: Resource Pages A–D and F.

Whole class work

- Read the book review of *The BFG* (Resource Page A) to your class and ask the children to think about the purpose and audience for this book review as you read it together again.

- After reading, ask the children to talk with their response partner about 'why' the book review would have been written and 'who' it might have been written for. Take feedback.

- It may be useful to mention that this review came from a web site – this will help the children to think about the possible audience.

- Discuss the organisation of the book review and use the responses to annotate the text (see Resource Page B) and start creating a checklist (see Resource Page F for ideas).

- Discuss the meaning of the words 'recommendation' and 'opinion'. It is important that these words are used in the context of this genre.

Independent, pair or guided work

- Using the review of *James and the Giant Peach* (Resource Page C), the children identify and annotate features from the checklist (see Resource Pages D and F).

Plenary

- Review the purpose and organisation of the book review studied in the independent work. ***Did you agree with the review? Why? What star rating would you give this book (or 'The BFG')?***

- ***Is there anything we could add to the checklist? Is there anything that we couldn't find in the new review?***

- The new review contains the word 'illustrator'. Discuss the meaning and add to the class checklist.

Writing an Introduction

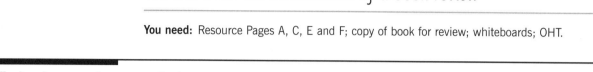

Objective

We will write the introduction of a book review

You need: Resource Pages A, C, E and F; copy of book for review; whiteboards; OHT.

Whole class work

- Review the previous day's work by discussing briefly the purpose and audience for book reviews.

- Ask the children to work with their response partner to remember five things that were on the checklist.

- Read the title and first sentence of the reviews of *The BFG* and *James and the Giant Peach* (Resource Pages A and C).

- Ask the children, with response partners, to identify three things that the two reviews have in common. Take feedback and annotate the texts to identify the language features. Add their responses to a class checklist (see Resource Page F for ideas).

- Using the checklist, model the opening of a book review for *The Diary of a Killer Cat* (Resource Page E).

- During the modelled writing, ensure that you:
  - refer constantly to the checklist and ask the children to indicate when they think you have used something on it
  - make deliberate errors for the children to identify and correct, for example, omit capital letters for names and titles and so on
  - reinforce learning about the size and proportion of capital letters
  - rehearse orally any ideas before putting them to paper
  - reread any writing and check for accuracy
  - demonstrate using a dictionary or other strategy to check a spelling
  - edit work as you are going.

- Involve the children by asking them to work with their response partner to suggest questions for the reader at the beginning of the review. Rehearse ideas and remind the children what the question is for before choosing one and writing it on the board.

Independent, pair or guided work

- It will be easier if all the children in the class write a review of the same book.

- Before writing the opening of the review, the children work with a response partner to write ideas for the opening question of their book review on a whiteboard.

- The children show their whiteboards, and selected pairs share their 'best' question. Use this assessment opportunity to identify children who need further help to form their opening question.

- The children write their opening using the modelled writing, your class checklist and the question already formed on their whiteboard as scaffolds.

- Select one or two children to write on an OHT.

Plenary

- Use the work on OHT to model checking the writing against your class checklist.

- The children then check their own or their partner's writing against the checklist.

Justifying Your Opinions

Objective

We will use the conjunction 'because' in sentences to explain why we like a part of the book or a character

You need: Resource Pages A–D and F; whiteboards.

Whole class work

- Read together the third and fourth paragraphs of the review of *The BFG* and the third paragraph of the *James and the Giant Peach* review (Resource Pages A and C).

- ***Do these paragraphs have anything in common?*** Encourage the children to discuss with their response partner. Take feedback, annotating the texts (see Resource Pages B and D) and adding to the class checklist (see Resource Page F for ideas).

- Before demonstrating the application of checklist features into the next paragraph of the book review, the children should discuss with their response partner:

> Why did you enjoy the book?
>
> Which was your favourite part and why?
>
> Which was your favourite character and why?

- When taking feedback, ensure that the children use 'because' in their sentence to justify their answer.

- Rehearse orally your response to these questions and use them as a framework for your modelled writing.

Independent, pair or guided work

- The children discuss with their response partner their favourite part and characters in the book they are reviewing.

- The children draft sentences on a whiteboard before they write the 'because' sentences in their review.

Plenary

- Select children to read aloud the beginning of their 'because' sentence and ask others to predict how the sentence will end. Check that the ideas in the 'because' sentences link.

- Ask the children to justify orally their favourite part or character in the story using 'because'.

Katie and Rachel's review

This review is from www.spaghettibookclub.com, an American site where children's book reviews are displayed. For the purpose of this resource, spelling has been Anglicised.

'The BFG' by Roald Dahl
Reviewed by Katie and Rachel (age 9)

Have you ever been woken up in the middle of the night frozen with fear because of a nightmare? If you have, you probably wish that someone would replace those horrifying nightmares for happy, delightful dreams. Well, in this story it really does happen. If you are lucky enough, the BFG might just do that for you.

Instead of going round in the middle of the night gobbling up humans, the BFG goes around and gives out good dreams. One night, after the BFG has given out dreams, he catches Sophie, a lonely orphan, getting a glimpse of him. Worried that Sophie will tell people what she has seen, he snatches her from out of her bedroom and scurries off with her to his cave.

Sophie and the BFG work hard together to get revenge on the giants for being greedy and selfish. Sophie and the BFG go through many exciting adventures together in this story including giving the Flesh Lump Eater (one of the man-eating giants) a dreadful nightmare!

I enjoyed this story very much because it is full of suspense and excitement. My favourite part is when Sophie and the BFG get their revenge on the giants and the BFG finally stands up to them. Roald Dahl's descriptive language, for example, "He yelled so loud that the heavens trembled," makes you feel like you are right there in the story. I also like how he makes up words like 'snozzcumber', which is a huge cucumber-shaped object that the BFG eats.

My favourite character is the BFG because he stands up for himself and helps other people to stand up for themselves too. This book reminds me of the 'The Twits' and 'Fantastic Mr Fox' which are both written by Roald Dahl, because they have the same message – if you're mean to someone, they might just get you back. Also, the books have someone that the main character has to stand up to.

I think you should join Sophie and the BFG in their exciting adventures because you never know what will happen next. I would recommend this book to anyone who likes adventures. I also think that if you like other Roald Dahl books you will like this book because they have very similar main ideas and writing styles. I think that this book will really inspire people to stand up for themselves like the BFG did.

I recommend this book for anyone aged from 7 to 10 years old.

I would give it a four star rating. ★★★★

(Exemplar analysis)

Example of analysis of Katie and Rachel's review

Title of book.

Author.

Reviewer's name and age.

Question to draw the reader in.

Verbs in the present tense.

Adjectives to describe characters.

Written in 1st person.

Sentences using 'because' to explain your opinion.

Why you enjoyed the book including favourite part and favourite character.

Reviewer talking to the reader.

Powerful verb to describe action.

Summary of the main events in the plot but not the ending.

Include names of main characters.

Use an example from the text to explain your point of view.

Suggest other similar books to the reader.

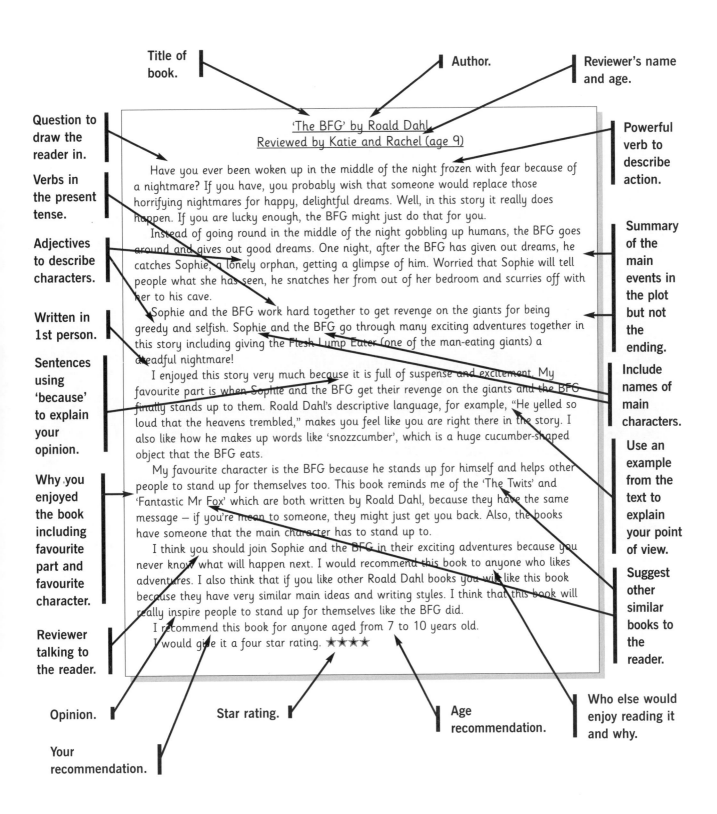

'The BFG' by Roald Dahl.
Reviewed by Katie and Rachel (age 9)

Have you ever been woken up in the middle of the night frozen with fear because of a nightmare? If you have, you probably wish that someone would replace those horrifying nightmares for happy, delightful dreams. Well, in this story it really does happen. If you are lucky enough, the BFG might just do that for you.

Instead of going round in the middle of the night gobbling up humans, the BFG goes around and gives out good dreams. One night, after the BFG has given out dreams, he catches Sophie, a lonely orphan, getting a glimpse of him. Worried that Sophie will tell people what she has seen, he snatches her from out of her bedroom and scurries off with her to his cave.

Sophie and the BFG work hard together to get revenge on the giants for being greedy and selfish. Sophie and the BFG go through many exciting adventures together in this story including giving the Flesh Lump Eater (one of the man-eating giants) a dreadful nightmare!

I enjoyed this story very much because it is full of suspense and excitement. My favourite part is when Sophie and the BFG get their revenge on the giants and the BFG finally stands up to them. Roald Dahl's descriptive language, for example, "He yelled so loud that the heavens trembled," makes you feel like you are right there in the story. I also like how he makes up words like 'snozzcumber', which is a huge cucumber-shaped object that the BFG eats.

My favourite character is the BFG because he stands up for himself and helps other people to stand up for themselves too. This book reminds me of the 'The Twits' and 'Fantastic Mr Fox' which are both written by Roald Dahl, because they have the same message – if you're mean to someone, they might just get you back. Also, the books have someone that the main character has to stand up to.

I think you should join Sophie and the BFG in their exciting adventures because you never know what will happen next. I would recommend this book to anyone who likes adventures. I also think that if you like other Roald Dahl books you will like this book because they have very similar main ideas and writing styles. I think that this book will really inspire people to stand up for themselves like the BFG did.

I recommend this book for anyone aged from 7 to 10 years old.
I would give it a four star rating. ★★★★

Opinion.

Your recommendation.

Star rating.

Age recommendation.

Who else would enjoy reading it and why.

(**Pupil copymaster**)

Jeffrey's review

<u>'James and the Giant Peach' by Roald Dahl, illustrated by Quentin Blake</u>

<u>Reviewed by Jeffrey (age 8)</u>

Have you ever been on an adventure that you'll never forget? James has. The story begins with a happy boy living on a beach with everything he wants and a mum and dad. What else could he want? Then it all falls apart.

James has to go and live on a tall hill with his aunts, one plump, one tall and skinny, and both mean. James is terrified of them and very unhappy. Then something surprising happens. A giant peach grows in the garden and that leads to James's happiness.

James meets some friends inside the peach, including a centipede, a spider and a ladybird and then the adventure starts!

I think this book is great because of the adventure that takes place. My favourite character is the centipede because he is always worried about all the feet he has. My favourite part is when he meets all the insects in the peach and travels with them.

I would recommend this book to people who like adventures or people who like books that make you have feelings, because this book makes you have many feelings while there is an adventure at the same time. Both boys and girls from Year 3 to Year 6 would enjoy this book.

I would give this book 9 out of 10.

(Exemplar analysis)

Example of analysis of Jeffrey's review

Title of the book with capital letters.

Author with capital letters.

Illustrator with capital letters.

Name of main character.

Question to draw the reader in.

Written in the present tense.

Written in the 1st person.

Why you enjoyed the book including favourite part and character.

Reviewer's name and age.

Adjectives to describe main characters.

Summary of the main parts of the story without giving away the ending.

Sentences using 'because' to explain your opinion.

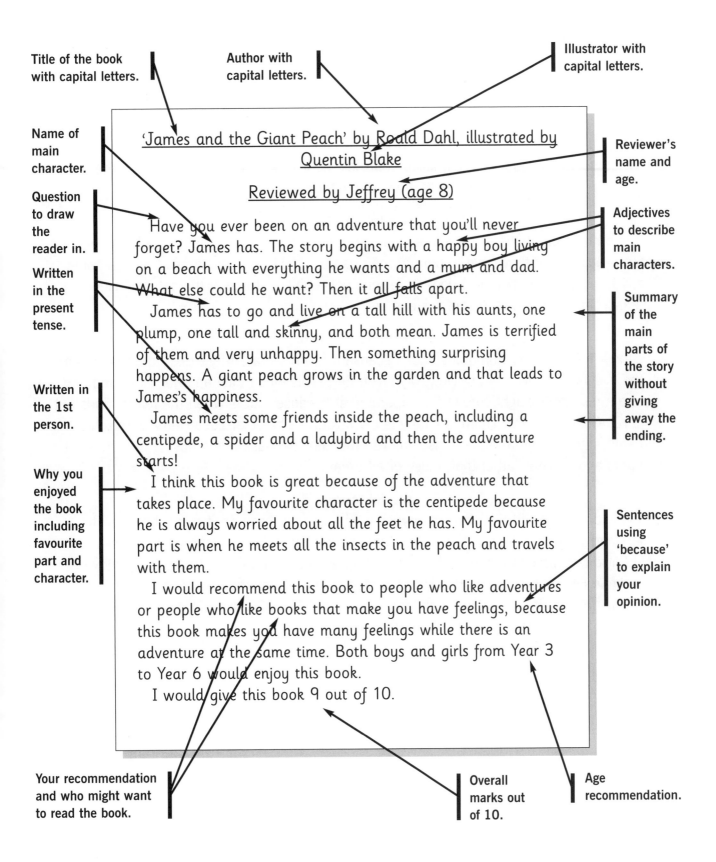

'James and the Giant Peach' by Roald Dahl, illustrated by Quentin Blake

Reviewed by Jeffrey (age 8)

Have you ever been on an adventure that you'll never forget? James has. The story begins with a happy boy living on a beach with everything he wants and a mum and dad. What else could he want? Then it all falls apart.

James has to go and live on a tall hill with his aunts, one plump, one tall and skinny, and both mean. James is terrified of them and very unhappy. Then something surprising happens. A giant peach grows in the garden and that leads to James's happiness.

James meets some friends inside the peach, including a centipede, a spider and a ladybird and then the adventure starts!

I think this book is great because of the adventure that takes place. My favourite character is the centipede because he is always worried about all the feet he has. My favourite part is when he meets all the insects in the peach and travels with them.

I would recommend this book to people who like adventures or people who like books that make you have feelings, because this book makes you have many feelings while there is an adventure at the same time. Both boys and girls from Year 3 to Year 6 would enjoy this book.

I would give this book 9 out of 10.

Your recommendation and who might want to read the book.

Overall marks out of 10.

Age recommendation.

(Exemplar material)

Modelled writing

‘The Diary of a Killer Cat’ by Anne Fine, illustrated by Steve Cox
Reviewed by: .... [teacher's name] (Age 21!)

Model for Day 1

What would you do if your cat killed your next-door neighbour's rabbit? This is the problem for Ellie, the soppy owner of Tuffy, the killer cat.

Model for Day 4

Tuffy thinks that he is just a normal cat, but Ellie is horrified that Tuffy is a killer. His first victim is a bird that they have to bury in their garden. Next he brings a dead mouse home. Finally he drags Thumper, next-door's precious pet rabbit, in through the cat flap! How are Ellie and her family going to sort this one out?

Model for Day 6

I think this is a very humorous book because it is written as Tuffy's diary and describes all the events from his point of view. My favourite part is when Ellie and her mum and dad meet the next-door neighbours in the supermarket because that is when the reader finds out what *really* happened to Thumper! Tuffy is my favourite character because he is mischievous and enjoys getting into trouble. I also enjoyed the book because it is amusing to read a cat's thoughts and feelings rather than those of a human.

Model for Day 7

I would recommend this book to anyone who has a cat because it might help you to understand your cat a little better and to think about things from a cat's point of view. I would also recommend this book to anyone who enjoys a humorous story or has enjoyed other Anne Fine books, like ‘Notso Hotso’ which is also a funny animal story.

In my opinion, it is suitable for children aged from 7 to 10 years old, but I think adults would also enjoy it because of the humour.

I would give this book a four star rating. ★★★★

(Exemplar material)

Checklist for reviewing books by the same author

Example of a checklist for text features of a book review

- Include the title of the book

- Include the author's name

- Include your name and age as the reviewer

- Write a summary of the plot of the story – not all of it, and without giving away the ending

- Introduce the main characters

- Say which is your favourite character and why

- Say which is your favourite part and why

- Give a recommendation – who else might like to read it and why

- Give a star rating

Example of a checklist for language features of a book review ②

- Use capital letters for the title of the book

- Use capital letters for the name of the author, reviewer and illustrator (if relevant)

- Use a question at the start of the review to draw the reader in and make them think – with a question mark at the end

- Write in paragraphs

- Write in the 1st person – use lots of 'I' and 'my'

- Write in the present tense

- Use sentences with 'because' in them to justify your opinion

- Use adjectives to describe the main characters

- Use powerful verbs to describe the action

(**Marking ladder**)

Name: _____

Pupil	Objective	Teacher
	My book review includes the title, the name of the author and the illustrator, with capital letters in the correct places.	
	I included my name and my age in brackets.	
	I used a question with a question mark at the beginning to interest the reader.	
	I wrote a short summary of the main events in the story, but did not include the ending.	
	I used adjectives to describe the main characters and powerful verbs to describe the action.	
	I used capital letters for the names of the main characters.	
	I used sentences with 'because' in them when giving my opinion.	
	I gave my recommendation.	
	I gave a star rating or marks out of ten.	
	I used the present tense.	
	I used the first person ('I', 'my', 'me' and so on).	
	What could I do to improve my book review next time?	

Letter Writing

Outcome

A letter (or email) to an author

Objectives

Sentence

3 to ensure grammatical agreement in speech and writing of pronouns and verbs, e.g. 'I am', 'we are', in standard English.

7 to become aware of the use of commas in marking grammatical boundaries within sentences.

Text

16 to read examples of letters written for a range of purposes, e.g., to recount, explain, enquire, complain, congratulate, comment; understand form and layout including use of paragraphs, ways of starting, ending, etc. and ways of addressing different audiences – formal/informal.

20 to write letters, notes and messages linked to work in other subjects, to communicate within school; letters to authors about books, selecting style and vocabulary appropriate to the intended reader.

21 to use IT to bring to a published form – discuss the relevance of layout, font, etc. to audience.

23 to organise letters into simple paragraphs.

Planning frame

- Understand the difference between formal and informal letters, when to use them and how to write them.

- Write letters in different styles for different audiences.

Notes

- Most children's authors are contactable by letter through their publishers, although replies often take some time. Many authors have their own web sites. The site **http://www.ukchildrensbooks.co.uk** provides links to many of these.

- This unit could be extended to writing letters to develop work across the curriculum for different audiences and purposes.

How you could plan this unit

Day 1	Day 2	Day 3	Day 4	Day 5
Reading	Reading and analysis	Reading and writing	Reading and analysis Read letter of enquiry (Resource Page M). Create checklist	Writing Compile questions to ask favourite author about specific books to put in letter. Research author on Internet
Different Types of Letters	*Formal Letters*	*Informal Replies*		

Day 6	Day 7	Day 8	Day 9
Reading and writing	Reading and writing Write middle paragraph of letter to author listing questions (Resource Page O)	Reading and writing Write final paragraph and close of letter to author	Evaluation Publish letter to author (using computer) and assess using marking ladder (Resource Page R)
The Opening			

Different Types of Letters

Objective

We will investigate the purpose and organisation of different types of letters

You need: Resource Pages A–F; a collection of different types of letters – mailshots from charities, private letters, emails, formal letters and so on.

Whole class work

- Discuss the range of letters the children may receive or send, including emails. Share the different types of letters you receive and send.

- Read aloud one or two letters. The children discuss with their response partner:
  - the purpose of the letter
  - who the letter is written for (with evidence).

- Read aloud the letter from Meeny, Miny, Mo & Co Solicitors (Resource Page A) and ask the children to identify the purpose and audience of the letter. Take feedback.

- Reread the letter and identify any words the children didn't understand or couldn't read, for example, 'solicitor', 'client', 'occupying', 'declined' and so on. Model strategies for decoding words and comprehending them, for example, reading on and working out the meaning of the word from the context.

- Discuss the formal language of the letter and how that is connected to the purpose (see Resource Page B). Demonstrate orally what it might sound like if written in informal language, to highlight the difference.

- Display the blank charts for recording audience and purpose (Resource Page C) and demonstrate completing the chart for the letter to Mr Wolf (Resource Page D).

Independent, pair or guided work

- Using the letter to the princess (Resource Page E), the children read and discuss the purpose and audience of the letter. The children make notes using their own copy of the chart.

Plenary

- Discuss the purpose of each of the letters and the formal or informal language used (see Resource Page F). The children give examples of the formal and informal language they identified.

- On a whiteboard, the children write 'I' on one side (for 'informal') and 'F' on the other (for 'formal'). Call out particular people you might write to and the children identify whether it should be a formal or an informal letter, for example:
  - a letter to your best friend
  - a letter to the Queen
  - a letter to a penpal
  - a note to your mum
  - a 'thank you' to Gran
  - a job application.

Formal Letters

Objective

We will investigate how a formal letter is organised and the language features that are used

You need: Resource Pages A, B, G, H and Q.

Whole class work

- Read together the letter to Mr Wolf (Resource Page A). Briefly review the purpose of the letter and the audience, which are the reasons for the formal language.

- With response partners, the children discuss the layout of the letter – how it is organised. ***How is the layout of the letter different from a story?***

- Use the responses from the discussion to annotate the letter (Resource Page B) and create a class checklist of the organisational features of a letter (see checklist 1, Resource Page Q for ideas).

- Ask the children to focus on the words and sentences used in the letter. Ask pairs of response partners to read one of the paragraphs and summarise what the paragraph is about. The children identify words that are 'formal'.

- Look at the middle paragraph. ***How many sentences are there?*** Answer: one. Do the same for other paragraphs.

- Use the ensuing discussion to annotate language features of the text and create a class checklist of language features (see checklist 2, Resource Page Q for ideas).

Independent, pair or guided work

- Read Resource Page G together before briefly discussing its purpose and audience.

- Using the annotated text (Resource Page H) and your class checklist, the children work to find the language and layout features.

Plenary

- With response partners, the children discuss whether they agree with the response from Mr Wolf's solicitor.

- ***How would you have responded?***

- Refer to your class checklist and select four of the features. Ask the children to stand in a particular corner of the room if they have annotated one of the four selected features. The children give examples.

- ***Are there any other features that we need to add to our checklist?***

Informal Replies

Objective

We will write a reply to a letter using an informal style

You need: Resource Pages A, I–L and Q.

Whole class work

- Read together Goldilocks' letter (Resource Page I) and discuss purpose and audience.

- The children discuss with response partners what makes it different from Resource Page A. Take feedback and use it to annotate the text (Resource Page J) and create a class checklist for an informal letter (see checklist 4, Resource Page Q for ideas).

- Note also that some features might remain the same, for example the use of the first person and the present tense.

- Use the incorrect spelling of 'porij' to work on the consonant cluster 'dge'. Ask the children to think of three words ending with the j phoneme, for example: 'edge', 'sledge', 'fridge'.

- Working with their response partners, the children imagine they were one of the bears and discuss what they might write in a reply to Goldilocks.

- Orally explain what you would write and why.

- Demonstrate writing a reply to Goldilocks (Resource Page K), using the features in checklist 4 (Resource Page Q). During the demonstration ensure that you:
  - reiterate the purpose, audience and organisation of the letter, for example, where to start when writing a letter by hand
  - refer constantly to the checklist
  - ask the children to indicate when you have used something on the checklist
  - plan content orally before writing and 'chunk' ideas into paragraphs
  - make deliberate errors for them to correct, for example, omit capitals for names
  - rehearse sentences orally before putting them to paper
  - reread and edit work as you are going
  - demonstrate using phonic strategies for spelling.

- To involve the children in the writing, ask them to work with their response partner to:
  - think of informal alternatives for ending the letter, for example, 'love from', 'best wishes', 'hope to see you soon', 'bye for now' and so on
  - suggest a postscript for the letter.

Independent, pair or guided work

- Working with a response partner or individually, the children write a reply to Goldilocks' letter of apology, using the class checklist and your modelled writing as support. Some children may benefit from using a writing frame.

Plenary

- Choose a few children to read their letters and ask the rest of the class to identify:
  - the purpose of the letter
  - the audience
  - the language the writer used to make it sound informal, rather than formal.

- On whiteboards, the children list people they might write to in an informal style.

- Make a list of informal ways of ending a letter.

The Opening

Objective

We will write the opening of a letter to a favourite author

You need: Resource Pages M, N, O and Q.

Whole class work

- This lesson assumes that the children are familiar with writing their own or the school's address. It may be necessary, before the lesson, to rehearse this skill. If, however, the letter is in the form of an email, then conventional address writing will not be necessary. Instead, any modelling should use the layout and conventions of an email. It is preferable for the children to compose both IT and handwritten letters and investigate the differences.

- Review Resource Page M. Discuss its purpose and audience and ask the children to think of three features that were on the class checklist for letters requesting information (created on Day 4, see page 129).

- Annotate the text (Resource Page N), indicating the features the children have remembered.

- Reveal the checklist for a formal letter (Resource Page Q) or your class checklist and review all the features.

- Remind the children of the questions they have written to ask an author about a particular book (Day 5 of this unit, see page 129). The children tell their response partner one of the questions. Share your own questions for the author as well.

- Demonstrate the opening of a letter to an author (Resource Page O), referring to the checklist. If the children are to produce this letter using IT, then the modelled writing should be carried out on a computer.

- During the demonstration writing ensure you reread and edit work as you are going, highlighting the word-processing features that are useful for editing. Ensure that the IT is supporting the literacy teaching and not the other way round.

- For safety reasons, it is advisable to use the school as the address of the sender, not the child's home.

Independent, pair or guided work

- Using the class checklist and your modelled example, the children write the opening paragraph of a letter to their selected author.

Plenary

- The children check their work against the class checklist and give examples of some of the features from their own work.

- Discuss what features of IT they used to help them lay out the letter correctly.

- ***When do you sign a formal letter 'Yours sincerely' and when do you use 'Yours faithfully'?*** Answer: 'sincerely' when you know the name of the person you are writing to; 'faithfully' if you have addressed the letter 'Sir or Madam'.

Dear Mr Wolf

& CO. SOLICITORS

Alley O Buildings, Toe Lane, Tel: 01234 567890

Dear Mr Wolf,

We are writing to you on behalf of our client, Miss Riding-Hood, concerning her grandma. Miss Hood tells us that you are presently occupying her grandma's cottage and wearing her grandma's clothes without this lady's permission.

Please understand that if this harassment does not cease, we will call in the Official Woodcutter, and – if necessary – all the King's horses and all the King's men.

On a separate matter, we must inform you that Messrs. Three Little Pigs Ltd. are now firmly resolved to sue for damages. Your offer of shares in a turnip or apple picking business is declined, and all this huffing and puffing will get you nowhere.

Yours sincerely,

Harold Meeny

H. Meeny

from The Jolly Pocket Postman, *A Ahlberg*

(Exemplar analysis)

Example of analysis of *Dear Mr Wolf*

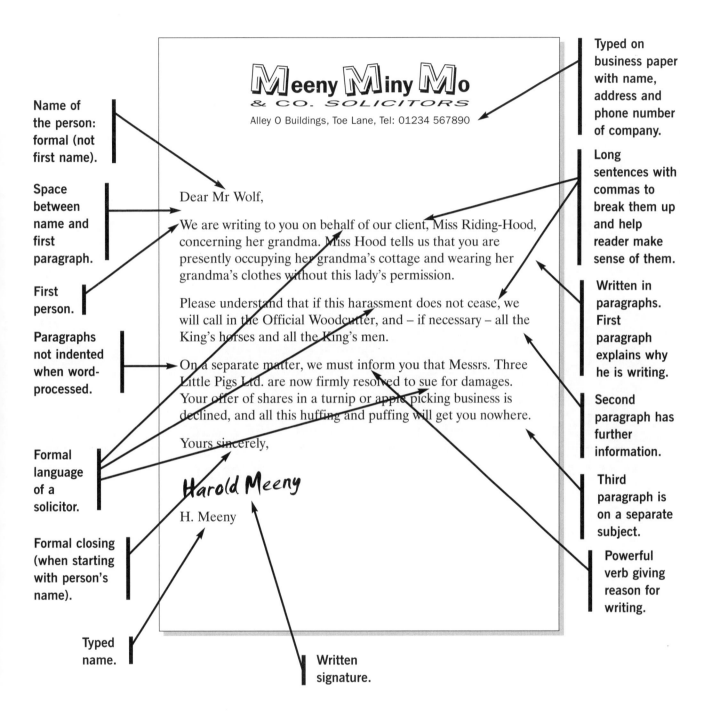

Typed on business paper with name, address and phone number of company.

Name of the person: formal (not first name).

Space between name and first paragraph.

First person.

Paragraphs not indented when word-processed.

Long sentences with commas to break them up and help reader make sense of them.

Written in paragraphs. First paragraph explains why he is writing.

Second paragraph has further information.

Third paragraph is on a separate subject.

Formal language of a solicitor.

Formal closing (when starting with person's name).

Powerful verb giving reason for writing.

Typed name.

Written signature.

Letter text

Dear Mr Wolf,

We are writing to you on behalf of our client, Miss Riding-Hood, concerning her grandma. Miss Hood tells us that you are presently occupying her grandma's cottage and wearing her grandma's clothes without this lady's permission.

Please understand that if this harassment does not cease, we will call in the Official Woodcutter, and – if necessary – all the King's horses and all the King's men.

On a separate matter, we must inform you that Messrs. Three Little Pigs Ltd. are now firmly resolved to sue for damages. Your offer of shares in a turnip or apple picking business is declined, and all this huffing and puffing will get you nowhere.

Yours sincerely,

Harold Meeny

H. Meeny

from The Jolly Pocket Postman, *A Ahlberg*

Audience and purpose chart blank

Letter	Audience	Purpose
1		
2		

(Exemplar material)

Audience and purpose chart

Letter	Audience	Purpose
1	Mr Wolf	• To inform and warn Mr Wolf that he will be in trouble if he doesn't move out of Grandma's house. • To inform him that the Three Little Pigs are suing him.
2		
3		

(Pupil copymaster)

Dear Princess

Dear Princess,

We at The Piper Press hope soon to publish a little book for younger readers in celebration of your recent marriage to H.R.H. Prince Charming. A copy of this book is enclosed for your approval.

We trust this somewhat shortened version of your Highness's most marvellous tale will not displease you. We also trust that you will be comfortable in your new home, and live happily ever after.

Your humble servant
(and loyal subject to be)

Peter Piper

Peter Piper
Managing Director

THE PETER PIPER PRESS • PECK PLACE • PICKLETON

from The Jolly Pocket Postman, *A Ahlberg*

Classworks Literacy Year 3 © Carolyn Bray, Nelson Thornes Ltd 2003

(Exemplar analysis)

Example of analysis of *Dear Princess*

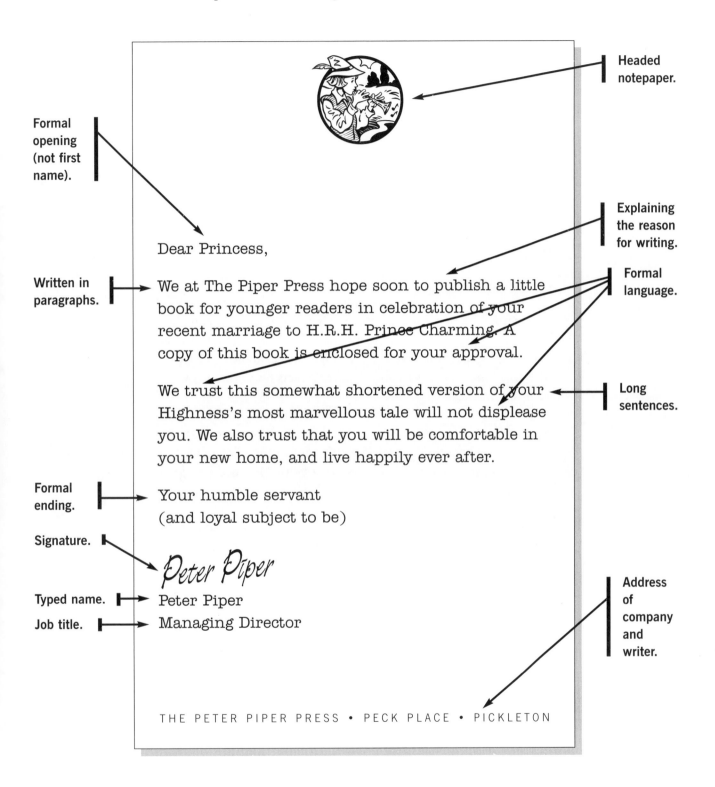

Headed notepaper.

Formal opening (not first name).

Dear Princess,

Explaining the reason for writing.

Formal language.

Written in paragraphs.

We at The Piper Press hope soon to publish a little book for younger readers in celebration of your recent marriage to H.R.H. Prince Charming. A copy of this book is enclosed for your approval.

We trust this somewhat shortened version of your Highness's most marvellous tale will not displease you. We also trust that you will be comfortable in your new home, and live happily ever after.

Long sentences.

Formal ending.

Your humble servant
(and loyal subject to be)

Signature.

Peter Piper

Typed name.

Peter Piper

Job title.

Managing Director

Address of company and writer.

THE PETER PIPER PRESS • PECK PLACE • PICKLETON

from The Jolly Pocket Postman, *A Ahlberg*

Classworks Literacy Year 3 © Carolyn Bray, Nelson Thornes Ltd 2003

(Pupil copymaster)

Dear Mr Meeny

Huff, Puff, Blow & Co.

Red Brick Building, Wood Lane, Strawbridge.
Telephone: 019876 543210 or Fax 019876 645310
www.huffpuffblow.co.uk

April 1st 2003

Reference: BBW / 1403

Dear Mr Meeny,

I am writing on behalf of my client, Mr B Wolf, to complain about the content of your latest correspondence to him. The letter contains a series of accusations for which you have no evidence. As his solicitor, I must insist you gather correct facts before wrongly accusing my client.

Mr Wolf assures me that he is not living in Grandma's cottage and has not been back to the area since the unfortunate incident. I must also inform you that my client has never worn Miss Riding-Hood's grandmother's clothing.

I must warn you and your client that if these false accusations do not cease, we will have no hesitation in taking the matter further.

Yours sincerely,

H. Puff

Mr H. Puff

from The Jolly Pocket Postman, *A Ahlberg*

Exemplar analysis

Example of analysis of *Dear Mr Meeny*

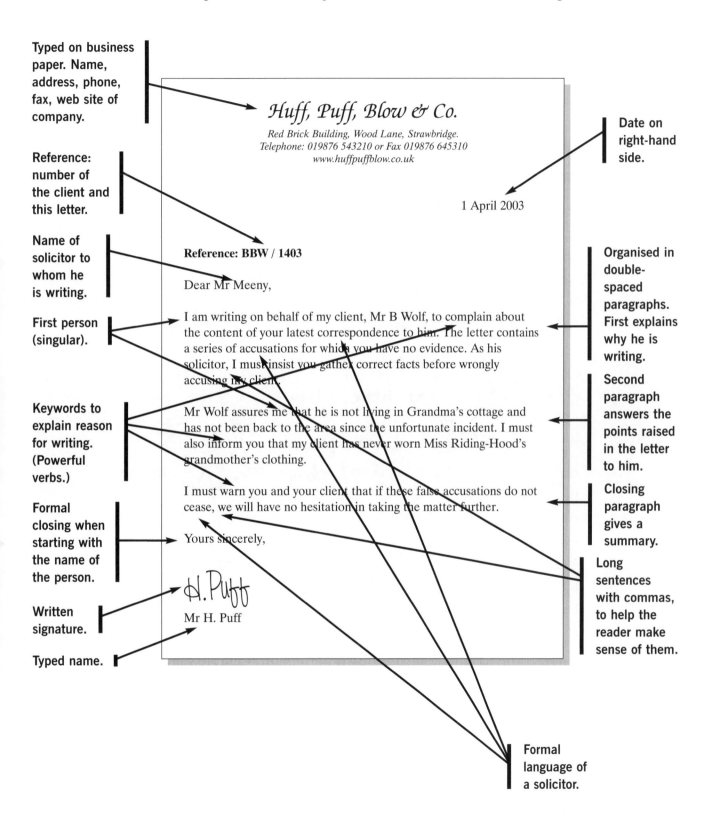

Typed on business paper. Name, address, phone, fax, web site of company.

Reference: number of the client and this letter.

Name of solicitor to whom he is writing.

First person (singular).

Keywords to explain reason for writing. (Powerful verbs.)

Formal closing when starting with the name of the person.

Written signature.

Typed name.

Date on right-hand side.

Organised in double-spaced paragraphs. First explains why he is writing.

Second paragraph answers the points raised in the letter to him.

Closing paragraph gives a summary.

Long sentences with commas, to help the reader make sense of them.

Formal language of a solicitor.

Huff, Puff, Blow & Co.
Red Brick Building, Wood Lane, Strawbridge.
Telephone: 019876 543210 or Fax 019876 645310
www.huffpuffblow.co.uk

1 April 2003

Reference: BBW / 1403

Dear Mr Meeny,

I am writing on behalf of my client, Mr B Wolf, to complain about the content of your latest correspondence to him. The letter contains a series of accusations for which you have no evidence. As his solicitor, I must insist you gather correct facts before wrongly accusing my client.

Mr Wolf assures me that he is not living in Grandma's cottage and has not been back to the area since the unfortunate incident. I must also inform you that my client has never worn Miss Riding-Hood's grandmother's clothing.

I must warn you and your client that if these false accusations do not cease, we will have no hesitation in taking the matter further.

Yours sincerely,

Mr H. Puff

from The Jolly Pocket Postman, *A Ahlberg*

Pupil copymaster

Dear Three Bears

Dear Mr and Mrs Bear
and Baby Bear,
I am very sory indeed that I
cam into your house
and ate Baby Bears
porij. Mummy says I am a bad girl.
I hardly eat any porij when she cooks
it she stays. Daddy says he will
mend the littel chair.

Love from
Goldilocks

P.S. Baby Bear can come to my
party if he likes. Then will be 3
kinds of jelly and a conjoora.

from The Jolly Pocket Postman, *A Ahlberg*

(Exemplar analysis)

Example of analysis of *Dear Three Bears*

There are spelling errors in the letter from Goldilocks – this, of course, is not a recognised feature of informal letters, however use the opportunity to talk about strategies to help with spelling.

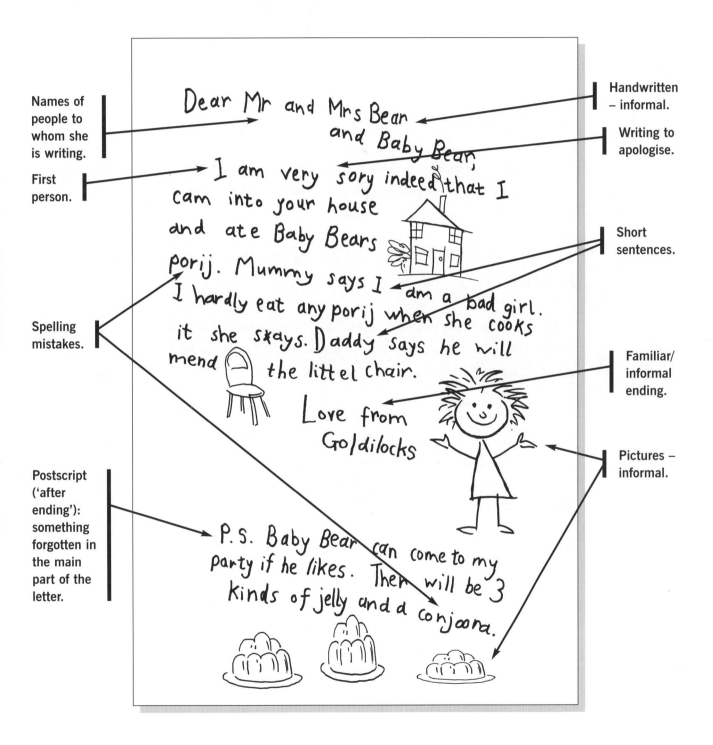

Names of people to whom she is writing.

First person.

Spelling mistakes.

Postscript ('after ending'): something forgotten in the main part of the letter.

Handwritten – informal.

Writing to apologise.

Short sentences.

Familiar/ informal ending.

Pictures – informal.

Dear Mr and Mrs Bean and Baby Bear,
I am very sory indeed that I cam into your house and ate Baby Bears porij. Mummy says I am a bad girl. I hardly eat any porij when she cooks it she stays. Daddy says he will mend the littel chair.
Love from Goldilocks
P.S. Baby Bear can come to my party if he likes. Ther will be 3 kinds of jelly and a conjoora.

from The Jolly Pocket Postman, *A Ahlberg*

(Pupil copymaster)

Dear Goldilocks

Three Bears' Cottage,
Big Wood,
Goldshire,
GD6 1TB.

5th March

Dear Goldilocks,

Thank you very much for your letter of apology, which we received yesterday. It was a pleasant surprise. Thank you also for inviting Baby Bear to your birthday party — he would love to come, as he loves jelly. Could you please let us know the date and time as soon as possible?

Daddy Bear has managed to fix Baby Bear's chair and it looks almost as good as new, so you can tell your Dad he doesn't need to worry about fixing it.

I must go and make the porridge for breakfast — I'll try not to make it too hot! Perhaps you might like to call round to visit us soon, when we're in, of course!

Best wishes,

Mummy Bear

PS: Maybe you should try a bowl of porridge for breakfast — it's very good for you.

from The Jolly Pocket Postman, *A Ahlberg*

(Exemplar analysis)

Example of analysis of *Dear Goldilocks*

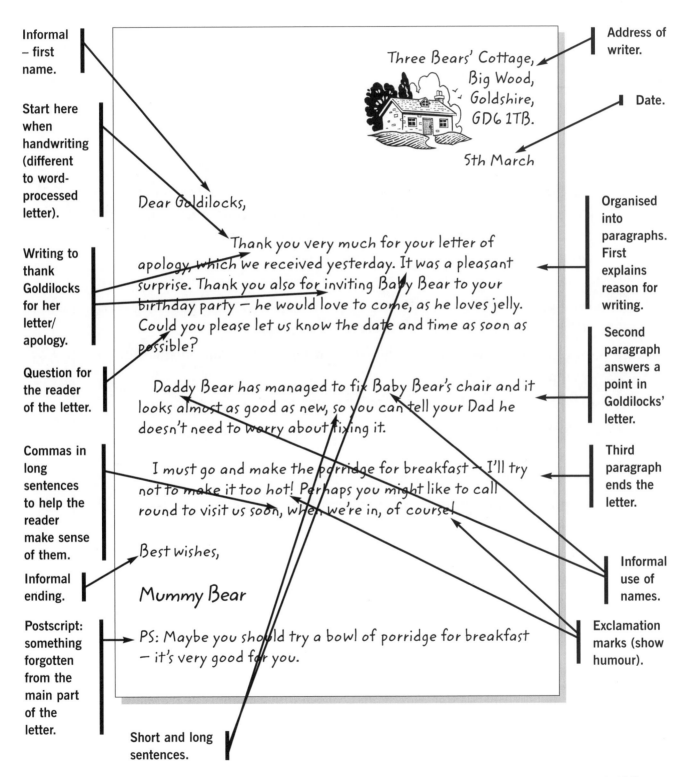

Informal – first name.

Start here when handwriting (different to word-processed letter).

Writing to thank Goldilocks for her letter/ apology.

Question for the reader of the letter.

Commas in long sentences to help the reader make sense of them.

Informal ending.

Postscript: something forgotten from the main part of the letter.

Short and long sentences.

Address of writer.

Date.

Organised into paragraphs. First explains reason for writing.

Second paragraph answers a point in Goldilocks' letter.

Third paragraph ends the letter.

Informal use of names.

Exclamation marks (show humour).

Three Bears' Cottage,
Big Wood,
Goldshire,
GD6 1TB.

5th March

Dear Goldilocks,

Thank you very much for your letter of apology, which we received yesterday. It was a pleasant surprise. Thank you also for inviting Baby Bear to your birthday party – he would love to come, as he loves jelly. Could you please let us know the date and time as soon as possible?

Daddy Bear has managed to fix Baby Bear's chair and it looks almost as good as new, so you can tell your Dad he doesn't need to worry about fixing it.

I must go and make the porridge for breakfast – I'll try not to make it too hot! Perhaps you might like to call round to visit us soon, when we're in, of course!

Best wishes,

Mummy Bear

PS: Maybe you should try a bowl of porridge for breakfast – it's very good for you.

from The Jolly Pocket Postman, *A Ahlberg*

Summer holiday enquiry

'Sea View'
19, Hall Walk,
Greater Fenwick,
TY6 9GK

15th February

Dear Sir or Madam,

Our family is planning to have a holiday in Scotland this summer, from 23rd May until 10th June. In order to help us make the most of our time in Scotland and to help us plan our itinerary, please would you be kind enough to send us some information?

We hope to spend at least ten days in the Western Highlands, so we would appreciate the following:

- A list of hotels and bed and breakfast accommodation for that area;
- Information on tourist attractions, particularly any to do with cycling;
- A map of the area;
- Ferry timetables for each of the islands;
- Any other information or brochures that we might find useful.

I enclose an SAE and look forward to receiving some useful information from you soon.

Yours faithfully,

Erica Poole

Erica Poole

(Exemplar analysis)

Example of analysis of *Summer holiday enquiry*

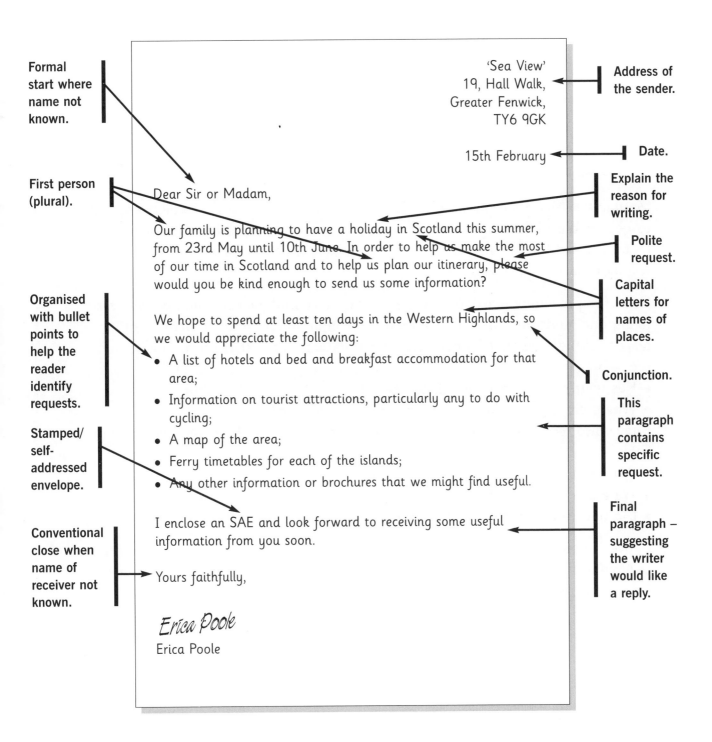

Formal start where name not known.

First person (plural).

Organised with bullet points to help the reader identify requests.

Stamped/ self-addressed envelope.

Conventional close when name of receiver not known.

'Sea View'
19, Hall Walk,
Greater Fenwick,
TY6 9GK

15th February

Dear Sir or Madam,

Our family is planning to have a holiday in Scotland this summer, from 23rd May until 10th June. In order to help us make the most of our time in Scotland and to help us plan our itinerary, please would you be kind enough to send us some information?

We hope to spend at least ten days in the Western Highlands, so we would appreciate the following:

- A list of hotels and bed and breakfast accommodation for that area;
- Information on tourist attractions, particularly any to do with cycling;
- A map of the area;
- Ferry timetables for each of the islands;
- Any other information or brochures that we might find useful.

I enclose an SAE and look forward to receiving some useful information from you soon.

Yours faithfully,

Erica Poole

Erica Poole

Address of the sender.

Date.

Explain the reason for writing.

Polite request.

Capital letters for names of places.

Conjunction.

This paragraph contains specific request.

Final paragraph – suggesting the writer would like a reply.

Letter to an author

Seaview School,
Green Road,
Porthmere,
Cornwall PL25 4RT
Tel: 01736 123454

6th June 2003

Dear Anne Fine,

My name is Mrs Bray and I am a teacher of a Year 3 class in Cornwall. I am writing to you because I have been reading several of your books and have really enjoyed them. I would like to ask you a few questions about your books which I hope you will be kind enough to answer.

One of my favourite books is 'The Diary of a Killer Cat', which I thought was very funny and made me laugh. I have read some information on your website, but I still have two questions that I would like you to answer about that book. The questions are:

• Has your cat ever done anything like Tuffy?
• Where did you get the idea for the character of Ellie?

I have also read 'The Angel of Nitshill Road' and 'Design a Pram' and would like to know:

• Why do you write so much about school?
• Were you ever bullied at school?
• Did you know someone bossy like Hetty in 'Design a Pram?'

I have written a book review of 'The Diary of a Killer Cat' that I have read to other children in the school during assembly to encourage them to read some of your books. I have enclosed the review and hope you enjoy reading it.

I hope you will answer my questions and I look forward to hearing from you soon.

Yours sincerely,

Carolyn Bray

Carolyn Bray

(Exemplar analysis)

Example of analysis of a letter to an author

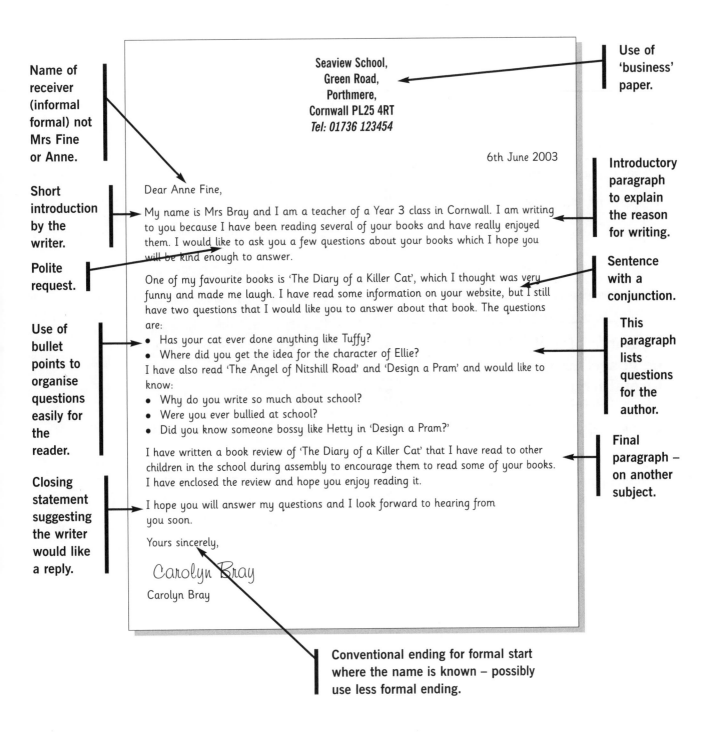

Name of receiver (informal formal) not Mrs Fine or Anne.

Short introduction by the writer.

Polite request.

Use of bullet points to organise questions easily for the reader.

Closing statement suggesting the writer would like a reply.

Seaview School,
Green Road,
Porthmere,
Cornwall PL25 4RT
Tel: 01736 123454

6th June 2003

Dear Anne Fine,

My name is Mrs Bray and I am a teacher of a Year 3 class in Cornwall. I am writing to you because I have been reading several of your books and have really enjoyed them. I would like to ask you a few questions about your books which I hope you will be kind enough to answer.

One of my favourite books is 'The Diary of a Killer Cat', which I thought was very funny and made me laugh. I have read some information on your website, but I still have two questions that I would like you to answer about that book. The questions are:

• Has your cat ever done anything like Tuffy?
• Where did you get the idea for the character of Ellie?

I have also read 'The Angel of Nitshill Road' and 'Design a Pram' and would like to know:

• Why do you write so much about school?
• Were you ever bullied at school?
• Did you know someone bossy like Hetty in 'Design a Pram?'

I have written a book review of 'The Diary of a Killer Cat' that I have read to other children in the school during assembly to encourage them to read some of your books. I have enclosed the review and hope you enjoy reading it.

I hope you will answer my questions and I look forward to hearing from you soon.

Yours sincerely,

Carolyn Bray

Carolyn Bray

Use of 'business' paper.

Introductory paragraph to explain the reason for writing.

Sentence with a conjunction.

This paragraph lists questions for the author.

Final paragraph – on another subject.

Conventional ending for formal start where the name is known – possibly use less formal ending.

Exemplar material

Checklists for letter writing

Example of a checklist for organisational features of a formal letter

- Put name and address of the sender at the top of the paper

- Write in paragraphs

- Start with 'Dear' and the person's name

- Leave spaces between the paragraphs

- Use 'Yours sincerely' (formal ending)

- Sign the letter by hand

- Type your name under the signature

Example of a checklist for language features of a formal letter

- Address the letter to 'Mr', 'Mrs' and so on (not first name) – formal

- In first paragraph explain why you are writing

- In second paragraph add further information

- Make third paragraph on another subject

- Use formal words

- Use long sentences with commas to break them up and help the reader make sense of them

- Use powerful verbs for effect

- Mostly write in the first person (plural)

- Mostly write in the present tense

Example of a checklist for a formal letter of enquiry

- Put your address at top right of page

- Use capital letters for people and places

- Give the date the letter was written

- Use 'Sir' or 'Madam', not a specific name

- Write a short sentence to introduce yourself

- Write in paragraphs:
  - in the first explain why you are writing
  - in the second set out your request
  - in the third suggest you expect a reply

- Use bullet points for requests

- Use long and short sentences, with conjunctions in long sentences

- Be polite

- Write in the first person

- Close using 'Yours faithfully'

Example of a checklist for an informal letter

- Write by hand

- Keep it to one paragraph

- Use short sentences

- Give a reason for writing – for example, to apologise

- Add a postscript (PS)

- Close with a familiar/informal ending – 'Love from'

- Write in the first person

(**Marking ladder**)

Name: _____

Pupil	Objective	Teacher
	In my letter to an author I wrote the school address on the right-hand side and put the date.	
	I addressed the author, followed by a comma.	
	In the first paragraph I introduced myself and explained why I am writing.	
	I asked questions in the second paragraph, using bullet points and ending with a question mark.	
	I explained about the book review in the third paragraph.	
	I wrote a closing statement asking for a reply.	
	I ended using 'Yours sincerely' or another formal ending.	
	I was polite ('please', 'thank you' and so on).	
	I used some short sentences and some long sentences using conjunctions, for example, 'because', 'but'.	
	I used the first person ('I', 'my' and so on).	
	I used the features on the toolbar to help me lay out the letter correctly, for example, use of bullet points, align right and so on.	
	I used capital letters for the names of people, places and titles.	
	What could I do to improve my letter next time?	

Poetry that Plays with Language

Outcome

A poem based on a real experience (visit, special event) that uses sound to create effects

Objectives	**Text**
	7 to select, prepare, read aloud and recite by heart poetry that plays with language or entertains; to recognise rhyme, alliteration and other patterns of sound that create effects.
	15 to write poetry that uses sound to create effects, e.g. onomatopoeia, alliteration, distinctive rhythms.

Planning frame	• Read a range of poems that are linked by use of language to create sound images.
	• Write in the style of one of the poems, using poetic techniques such as alliteration and onomatopoeia.

Notes	• This unit will be most effective if the children have collected onomatopoeia or made sound recordings of a visit or special event. They will need to use their own collection of onomatopoeia to write their own poem.
	• This unit only deals with one form of poetry from the text range for term 3. The children should also explore forms of humorous poetry, e.g. joke poems, nonsense verse, riddles and so on which do not require a written outcome.

How you could plan this unit

Day 1	Day 2	Day 3	Day 4	Day 5
Reading	**Speaking and listening** Groups perform a poem from previous lesson	**Reading** Focus on onomatopoeia. Read Resource Pages G, H and I and/or review own onomatopoeia from class visit or event	**Speaking and listening and writing**	**Writing** The children write next two lines
Language Effects			*Sound Effects*	

Day 6	Day 7	Day 8
Writing	**Writing** The children edit poems and publish (using IT)	**Performance** The children perform own poems in pairs or small groups. Record using video or audio tape
Writing a Poem		

Language Effects

Objective

We will identify how a poet uses language to create effects for the reader

You need: Resource Pages A–F and J; individual whiteboards and pens.

Whole class work

- Read Resource Page A aloud to the children. Discuss what a 'sampan' is and if possible show a picture. Read the poem again and ask the children to close their eyes and visualise the picture the words are creating. Allow two minutes to sketch on a whiteboard what they can 'see'. Ask them to discuss their pictures with a response partner.

- Read the poem as a class. The children discuss with their response partner what their favourite line is and why.

- Take feedback and focus on the language choices and the rhythm the poet has used.

- Use syllable counting to explore the use of rhythm.

- Use the children's responses to annotate the text and create a class checklist (see Resource Pages B and J for ideas).

- Note the poem's pattern:

  > - repeat of the first four lines at the end
  > - repeat of lines 6 and 8
  > - three syllables in line 1 and four syllables in lines 2–4
  > - eight syllables in lines 5–8

- Go through the same procedure of reading, visualising and exploring Resource Page C. In pairs, the children find two similarities and two differences between the poems. Use their responses to annotate *Waterfall* (see Resource Page D) and add other features to your class checklist.

Independent, pair or guided work

- The children investigate *Windy Nights* (Resource Page E) and annotate with any of the features in the class checklist (also see Resource Page F).

- ***Sketch a scene from the poem that you think the poet is trying to represent.***

Plenary

- Discuss which checklist features were used in *Windy Nights*. ***Are there any others to add?***

- Read each of the poems aloud as a class and ask the children to discuss with their response partner which poem uses sound most effectively and why. Take feedback.

- Summarise what language features poets use to create effects.

Sound Effects

Objective

We will use language features to create sound effects for our own poem

You need: Resource Pages A and J; individual whiteboards; OHP or whiteboard; flip chart.

Whole class work

- Review the previous day's lesson by giving the children one minute to write as many examples of onomatopoeia as possible on whiteboards. Some children may prefer to work in pairs.

- Review the definition of onomatopoeia and its effect.

- If possible, take the children outside and working in pairs, spend five minutes listening and noting down examples of onomatopoeia for sounds that they hear, for example, traffic, voices, birds, radios, music, sirens and so on.

- Take feedback and list onomatopoeia (including your own ideas) on a flip chart, grouping them to match the nouns they are describing, for example, 'shrieking sirens'.

- Refer back to *Sampan* (Resource Page A) and review the structure of the poem, particularly the first two lines.

- Use the modelled writing (Resource Page J) to demonstrate using the nouns and onomatopoeia collected.

- *Sampan* rhymes on every line. The children will get distracted from using effective language if they are required to make the poem rhyme as well.

- During the modelled writing ensure you:
  - explain orally your choice of words
  - orally rehearse ideas before committing them to paper
  - refer to your class checklist
  - ask the children to indicate when they see you use something from the checklist
  - constantly edit your work
  - model more than one variation of the two lines, indicating that you might decide when you've written the other lines
  - ask the children to close their eyes and visualise as you read your ideas. ***Do the words create the sound effect?***

Independent, pair or guided work

- Using their own collection of onomatopoeia, the class checklist and the modelled writing, the children work on whiteboards or in rough books to develop ideas for the first two lines of their poem based on *Sampan*.

Plenary

- Use the children's ideas and check them against the checklist. ***What onomatopoeia have you used? Who has used some alliteration?***

- Use one or two examples to demonstrate how to improve work using a response sandwich: one good comment; one area for improvement; another good comment.

- Ask the children to comment on whether the language used creates a sound effect.

Writing a Poem

Objective

We will use language effects to write poetry describing sound

You need: Resource Pages A and J; OHTs.

Whole class work

- Reread *Sampan* (Resource Page A), focusing on the four middle lines. Draw attention to:

  - powerful verbs
  - adjectives
  - repeating lines 6 and 8
  - description of location

- In pairs, the children think of two or three adjectives that would describe the place where their poem is set.

- This could be a good opportunity for the children to use a thesaurus.

- Take feedback and review the function of the adjective. The children share adjectives that could be used for their poems.

- Model writing four lines for the next part of your poem (see Resource Page J). *Do the words create the sound effect?*

- As the children have collected a number of examples of onomatopoeia, it will be effective to use appropriate onomatopoeia for lines 6 and 8.

Independent, pair or guided work

- Using your class checklist and the modelled writing, the children experiment with writing four lines of their own poem, with lines 6 and 8 repeating.

- Select one or two children to work on an OHT.

Plenary

- Use the children's work on OHT to demonstrate checking against the checklist for language features.

- Ask the children to suggest alternative adjectives and onomatopoeia for the lines to produce a contrasting effect for the modelled writing, for example, the street at night might be described as:

  > Up and down the silent street
  > Whisper scurry hush and creep
  > Cats, mice and foxes meet
  > Whisper scurry hush and creep

- Ask the children to rate their own work using a scale of 1 to 5 according to whether the language they have used creates the effect they want.

Sampan

Waves lap lap

Fish fins clap clap

Brown sails flap flap

Chopsticks tap tap

Up and down the long green river

Ohe Ohe lanterns quiver

Willow branches brush the river

Ohe Ohe lanterns quiver

Waves lap lap

Fish fins clap clap

Brown sails flap flap

Chopsticks tap tap

Tao Lang Pee

Glossary

Sampan = small boat with single oar at the stern, used in the Far East

Ohe lanterns = paper lanterns

(Exemplar analysis)

Example of analysis of *Sampan*

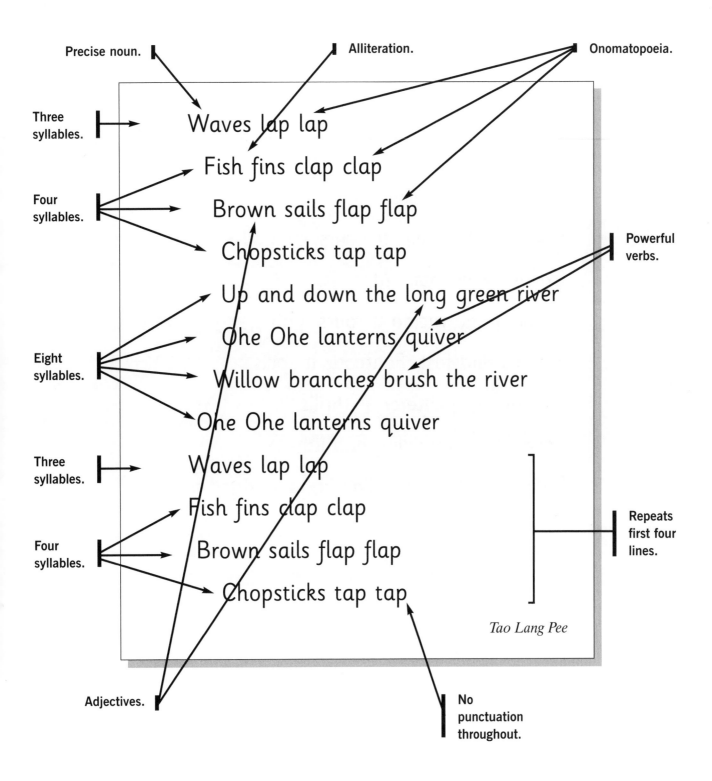

Precise noun.

Alliteration.

Onomatopoeia.

Three syllables.

Waves lap lap

Fish fins clap clap

Four syllables.

Brown sails flap flap

Chopsticks tap tap

Powerful verbs.

Up and down the long green river

Ohe Ohe lanterns quiver

Eight syllables.

Willow branches brush the river

Ohe Ohe lanterns quiver

Three syllables.

Waves lap lap

Fish fins clap clap

Four syllables.

Brown sails flap flap

Chopsticks tap tap

Repeats first four lines.

Tao Lang Pee

Adjectives.

No punctuation throughout.

Classworks Literacy Year 3 © Carolyn Bray, Nelson Thornes Ltd 2003

(Pupil copymaster)

Waterfall

Water white as a veil,

Arches across rocks, falls,

Tosses in turbulent torrents,

Excites, enchants, enthralls.

Rushing and racing it roars, pours,

Furious and fast. Fantastic it spills

Amazingly splintered it thrills.

Leaps, light-sparkling and lithe.

Lands and lingers in limpid, lace-edged pools.

Cynthia Rider

(Exemplar analysis)

Example of analysis of *Waterfall*

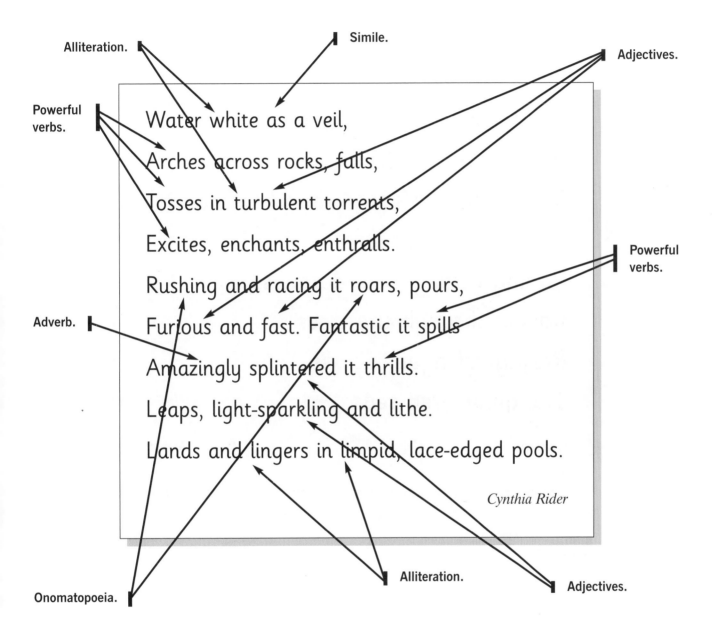

Alliteration.

Simile.

Adjectives.

Powerful verbs.

Water white as a veil,

Arches across rocks, falls,

Tosses in turbulent torrents,

Excites, enchants, enthralls.

Rushing and racing it roars, pours,

Powerful verbs.

Adverb.

Furious and fast. Fantastic it spills

Amazingly splintered it thrills.

Leaps, light-sparkling and lithe.

Lands and lingers in limpid, lace-edged pools.

Cynthia Rider

Onomatopoeia.

Alliteration.

Adjectives.

(Pupil copymaster)

Windy Nights

Rumbling in the chimneys,

Rattling at the doors,

Round the roofs and round the roads

The rude wind roars;

Raging through the darkness,

Raving through the trees,

Racing off again across

The great grey seas.

Rodney Bennett

(Exemplar analysis)

Example of analysis of *Windy Nights*

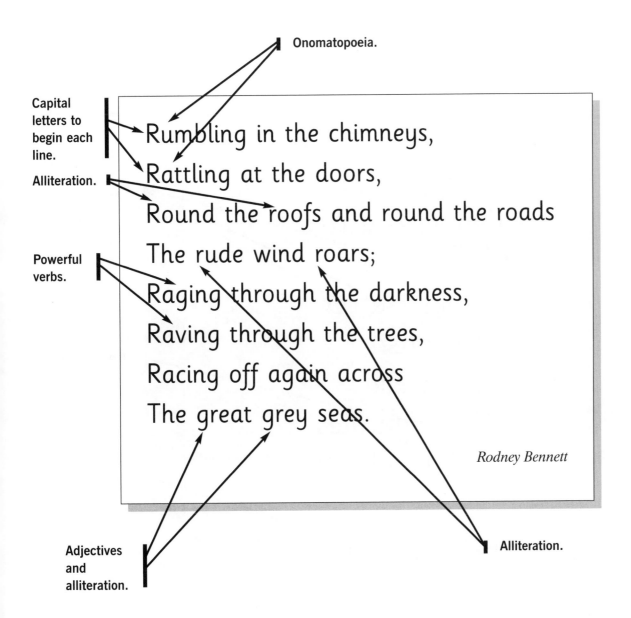

Onomatopoeia.

Capital
letters to
begin each
line.

Alliteration.

Powerful
verbs.

Rumbling in the chimneys,

Rattling at the doors,

Round the roofs and round the roads

The rude wind roars;

Raging through the darkness,

Raving through the trees,

Racing off again across

The great grey seas.

Rodney Bennett

Adjectives
and
alliteration.

Alliteration.

(Exemplar analysis)

Example of analysis of *Kitchen Sounds*

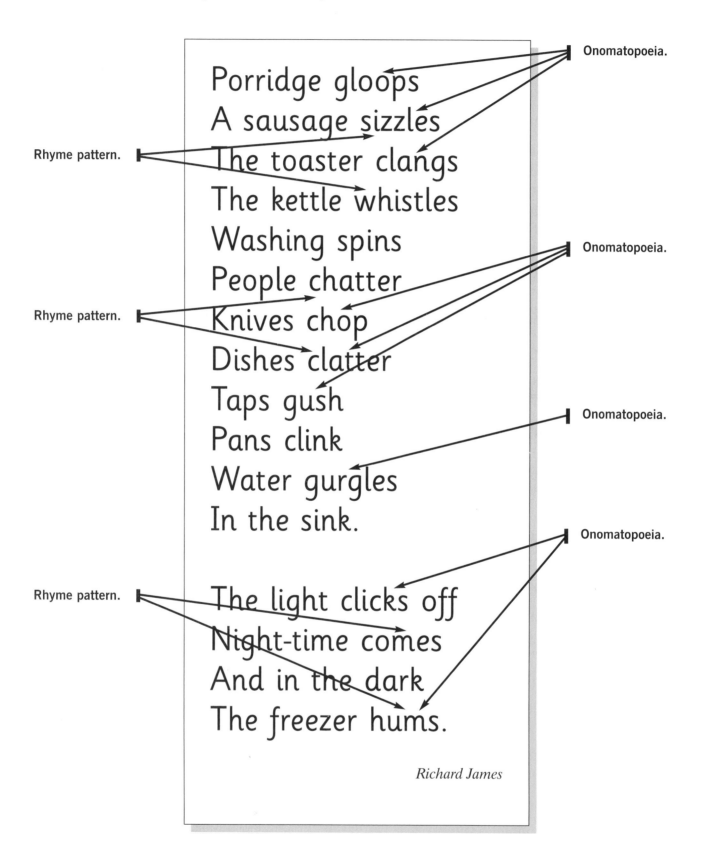

Onomatopoeia.

Porridge gloops
A sausage sizzles
The toaster clangs
The kettle whistles
Washing spins
People chatter
Knives chop
Dishes clatter
Taps gush
Pans clink
Water gurgles
In the sink.

The light clicks off
Night-time comes
And in the dark
The freezer hums.

Richard James

Rhyme pattern.

Onomatopoeia.

Onomatopoeia.

Onomatopoeia.

(Exemplar analysis)

Example of analysis of *Metal Fettle*

ABCB rhyme pattern.

Onomatopoeia.

The clank of a tank *a*
the chink of chains *b*
the tinkle of tins *c*
the rattle of trains. *b*

Onomatopoeia.

The click of a clasp
the clang of a bell
the creak of a hinge
the chime of a spell.

Not much punctuation.

Onomatopoeia.

The shatter of cymbals
the clash of swords
the clatter of cutlery
the twang of chords.

Onomatopoeia.

The ping of keys
the song of a wheel
the plink of pans
the ring of steel.

John Rice

(Exemplar analysis)

Example of analysis of *The Sound Collector*

A stranger called this morning
Dressed all in black and grey
Put every sound into a bag
And carried them away.

The whistling of the kettle
The turning of the lock
The purring of the kitten
The ticking of the clock
The popping of the toaster
The crunching of the flakes
When you spread the marmalade
The scraping noise it makes
The hissing of the frying pan
The ticking of the grill
The bubbling of the bathtub
As it starts to fill
The drumming of the raindrops
On the window pane
When you do the washing up
The gurgle of the drain
The crying of the baby
The squeaking of the chair
The swishing of the curtain
The creaking of the stair

A stranger called this morning
He didn't leave his name
He left us only silence
Life will never be the same.

Roger McGough

Rhyme scheme.

Alliteration.

No use of full stops or commas in this section of the poem.

Onomatopoeia.

Many lines follow the same format, 'The ... of the ...'.

Capital letters at the beginning of every line.

(Exemplar material)

Checklist and model for poetry that plays with language

Example of a checklist for writing a poem

- Use onomatopoeia
- Use alliteration
- Use adjectives
- Use powerful verbs
- Use a rhyming pattern
- Pay attention to pace and rhythm
- Use punctuation to help meaning – commas and full stops
- Use adverbs
- Use similes or other imagery

Example of modelled writing based on *Sampan*

Bikes zoom zoom
Buses beep beep
Wet wheels splash, splash
Car doors slam slam
Up and down the crowded street
Thunder rumble roar and screech
Lorries cars and people meet
Thunder rumble roar and screech
Bikes zoom zoom
Buses beep beep
Wet wheels splash, splash
Car doors slam slam

(Marking ladder)

Name: _____

Pupil		Teacher
	My poem uses onomatopoeia and alliteration to create sound effects.	
	I have included adjectives to describe.	
	I have used syllables to help me think about the rhythm.	
	I have repeated lines 6 and 8 using onomatopoeia.	
	I have repeated the first 4 lines.	
	I have used rhyme if appropriate.	
	I have performed my poem making use of the words as sound effects.	
	I have published my poem.	
	What could I do to improve my poem next time?	

Adventure Stories

Outcome

An adventure story in chapters

Objectives

Sentence

4 to use speech marks and other dialogue punctuation appropriately in writing and to use the conventions which mark boundaries between spoken words and the rest of the sentence.

Text

1 to retell main points of story in sequence; to compare different stories; to evaluate stories and justify their preferences.

2 to refer to significant aspects of the text, e.g. opening, build-up, atmosphere, and to know language is used to create these, e.g. use of adjectives for description.

10 to plot a sequence of episodes modelled on a known story, as a plan for writing.

11 to write openings to stories or chapters linked to or arising from reading; to focus on language to create effects, e.g. building tension, suspense, creating moods, setting scenes.

13 to write more extended stories based on a plan of incidents and set out in simple chapters with title and author details; to use paragraphs to organise the narrative.

Planning frame

- Identify and understand the techniques used in suspense/adventure writing.
- Write own suspense/adventure story.
- Edit and publish using IT.

Note

- The children will need additional time to publish their story using IT, including a title page and author details, then evaluate it against the marking ladder criteria.

How you could plan this unit

Day 1	Day 2	Day 3	Day 4	Day 5
Reading	**Reading** Read remainder of *House Haunting*. Complete story map	**Writing**	**Reading** Read story opening of *House Haunting*. Create checklist	**Sentence work** Speech (*Grammar for Writing* Unit 16)
What Happens Next?		*Planning a Story*		

Day 6	Day 7	Day 8	Day 9	Day 10
Writing	**Reading**	**Reading**	**Writing** The children write build-up in chapter 2	**Reading**
The Opening	*The Build-up*	*Creating Suspense*		*The Climax*

Day 11	Day 12	Day 13	Day 14	Day 15
Writing	**Reading** The children read resolution and create checklist	**Writing** The children write resolution in chapter 4	**Reading** The children read ending and create checklist	**Writing** The children write ending in chapter 5
Writing a Climax				

What Happens Next?

Objective

We will retell the main points of a story and predict what might happen next

You need: Resource Pages A–C; flip chart; individual whiteboards and pens.

Whole class work

- Briefly discuss the genre of adventure stories. *Have you read any adventure stories? What sort of things would you expect to happen in an adventure story?*

- Discuss the title of Resource Page A, *House Haunting*, and how this affects readers' expectations. *Can you predict what the story might be about from the title?*

- Read together chapters 1, 2 and half of chapter 3 (up to '... the door was stuck fast'), stopping at various places to ask the children to predict what might happen next and to discuss the meaning of particular words, for example, 'destination', 'briar', 'weed-infested' (see Resource Pages A–C).

- After reading, discuss: *What do we know about the characters so far?* Use this discussion to make the point that the author doesn't *tell* the reader that Ben is the brave one, but instead *shows* the reader. Ask the children to point out where the author does this.

- *How does the author make the reader want to read on?* Answer: using suspense at the end of a chapter. Ask the children to identify use of suspense so far.

- In pairs, the children think of three things that have happened in the story so far and put them in the correct chronological order. Take some feedback.

- On the flip chart, draw a sketch of the opening scene: Ben's house, Ben and Jack leaving, Mum carrying shopping. The children tell the story from the picture. *Where do Ben and Jack go next on their adventure? And after that?* Continue in this way, making notes on the flip chart of the sequence of places and events in the story so far.

Independent, pair or guided work

- The children work in pairs to create a story map of the main event and places in the story so far.

Plenary

- Ask one or two pairs to retell part of the story from their story map.

- Ask pairs to predict what the next picture would be and draw it on their whiteboard. Compare predictions.

Planning a Story

Objective

We will plan our own adventure story

You need: Resource Pages M, N and Q; OHT.

Whole class work

- Using an OHT of Resource Page M, display the 'opening' section only of the story hill. Read together and ask the children to predict what might be written in the 'build-up' box.

- Display the build-up box and ask them to predict what would be in the 'climax' box and so on, until the whole story hill is displayed.

- If the language of story structure – opening, build-up, climax, resolution, ending – is unfamiliar to some, ensure that this is covered as you go through the story hill.

- On your flip chart, draw a story hill and use it to demonstrate how to plan an adventure story (see Resource Page Q).

- During the modelled writing of the plan make sure you:
  - orally explain the 'big picture' of the story first before noting it on the hill
  - make sure that you speak your ideas aloud before noting them – emphasise that planning is about thinking, not about writing
  - explain the use of notes (not sentences) when planning
  - don't plan chronologically – often the idea for the climax comes before the build-up and so on
  - keep rereading your work and retelling the story from your notes to check for coherence
  - point out the need for planning before writing, for example, if the children are to be rescued by a dog, then the writer needs to include a dog at the beginning
  - make explicit things that are implicit, for example, the story starts at the campsite, but then moves to the woods; the specific characteristics of the characters – one brave, one nervous
  - build in opportunities for suspense at the end of chapters and discuss and plan how the suspense will be resolved at the beginning of the next chapter
  - include your class in aspects of the planning, for example, ideas on how the characters could be rescued.

Independent, pair or guided work

- Using the blank story hill (Resource Page N), the children work in pairs or individually to plan their own adventure story. They may use written notes or pictures on their plan.

- Some children may benefit from working as a group with a scribe.

Plenary

- Ask the children to tell a part of their story (opening, resolution and so on) from their plan, to their response partner.

- Check story plans by selecting children to explain various elements of their plan. *What are the characters warned not to do? Who is the brave character and who is the nervous one? Where does the adventure happen?*

- Ask the children to think of the opening line for their story. *What are the characters warned not to do and who warns them?*

The Opening

Objective

We will write the opening to our adventure story

You need: Resource Pages O–Q and V.

Whole class work

- Ask the children to discuss with their response partner what language features were found in the opening of the adventure story. Take feedback and ask the children to give examples of particular features to check their understanding (see Resource Page P for ideas).

- Refer to the story hill modelled previously (Resource Page Q) and read the notes. Orally demonstrate turning some of the notes into sentences.

- Compile a class checklist (see checklist 1, Resource Page V for ideas).

- Ask the children to work with their response partners to construct the start of their own story using speech with a warning given by an adult. Take feedback and use ideas to construct the opening line of your adventure story.

- Model the rest of the story opening (see Resource Pages O and P) ensuring that you:
  - refer to the checklist and ask the children to identify when you have used something on the checklist
  - orally rehearse sentences before putting them to paper
  - explain explicitly how your choice of words, particularly powerful verbs, shows the reader a lot about the character
  - make occasional deliberate mistakes, for example, in spelling and punctuation, to highlight and correct any misconceptions
  - explain orally any decisions you make as a writer, for example, the choice of one powerful verb over another
  - refer to the planning notes
  - involve the children in giving suggestions, such as examples of powerful verbs.

Independent, pair or guided work

- Before the children work independently, they discuss their story opening with response partners and help each other to construct the first sentence for their story opening, using speech by one character to warn the others.

- Using the modelled writing (Resource Page P), your class checklist, and their plans on the story hill as support, the children write the opening of their adventure story.

Plenary

- Select some children to read out their openings and check them against your class checklist.

- Ask the class to predict what the ending of the stories will be from the beginnings they hear.

- Emphasise the importance of knowing how your story will end when you start to write it.

The Build-up

Objective

We will investigate what language features an author uses when writing the build-up to a story

You need: Resource Pages B, H, R, S and V.

Whole class work

- Read the build-up of *House Haunting* together (Resource Page B). With response partners, the children discuss which was their favourite sentence and why. Take some feedback.

- Together, read the extract to 'up the groaning staircase'. Ask the children to shut their eyes and listen out for the words that help paint a picture in their minds. Take some feedback and annotate the text (see Resource Page H) to include words identified in their responses.

- Use further questioning to identify the language features used to describe the setting. **What did the boys hear/smell/see in the house? What time of year do you think it was? Why?**

- Annotate the text with the features and create a class checklist (see checklist 2, Resource Page V for ideas).

- Reread the final paragraph of the build-up, 'Suddenly' to 'back down the stairs'. **What do you notice about some of the sentences in this paragraph?** Answer: they are very short, which creates suspense.

- Together, identify the language features used to create suspense. Annotate the text and create a class checklist (see checklist 2, Resource Page V for ideas).

Independent, pair or guided work

- Using one of the extracts on Resource Page R, the children work individually or in pairs to annotate the text, identifying the features on the class checklist (see also Resource Page S).

Plenary

- Ask the children to give examples from their texts of the features identified on the checklist, focusing on those that describe the setting and those for writing suspense.

- Read the suspense paragraph from one of the extracts. The children discuss what they think might happen next in the story. Take feedback.

- Discuss why authors use suspense writing at the end of a chapter.

Creating Suspense

Objective

We will identify language features used for suspense writing and use them in our own writing

You need: Resource Pages H and T–V; highlighters; OHTs.

Whole class work

- In pairs, the children recall the features from the checklist that were used to create suspense. Take feedback.

- Display the annotated text from the previous lesson (Resource Page H). Reread the suspense paragraph and review the checklist features.

- Introduce Resource Page T, as another example of suspense writing. Read the text together.

- In pairs, the children annotate the text with any language features used to increase suspense. Take feedback and annotate features (see Resource Page U).

- Create a class checklist for suspense writing including the features from the 'build-up' checklist from the previous lesson (see also Resource Page V).

- Using your class checklist, model a short piece of suspense writing:

> Suddenly I heard it. It came from outside my bedroom door. I lay in bed, frozen with fear. What was it? I gripped the duvet cover. Silence. A shiver crept down my spine. Something or someone was outside my bedroom door.

- During the modelling of writing ensure you:
  - refer to your class checklist
  - orally explain all decisions about word and sentence choice
  - orally rehearse sentences before putting them to paper
  - constantly reread your work and make improvements
  - ask the children to identify when you have used something from the checklist.

Independent, pair or guided work

- Using your checklist and the modelled writing as a support, the children work in pairs or individually to write their short piece of suspense writing. Select one or two children to write on an OHT.

Plenary

- Use the work on the OHT to demonstrate checking the writing against the class checklist.

- The children use highlighters or underlining to annotate their work against the class checklist.

- The children share work with their response partner and discuss ways to improve it using a response sandwich: one good comment; one area for improvement; another good comment.

The Climax

Objective

We will identify the features that authors use when writing the climax of the story

You need: Resource Pages C, I and V.

Whole class work

- Ask the children to talk with response partners about the events in *House Haunting* so far. Take feedback to check that they have the sequencing in the correct order.

- Discuss what is meant by the 'climax' of the story. Explain that it contains all the problems and action that happen before the climax (the top of the story hill).

- Read the first half of chapter 3 (Resource Page C) together and ask the children to identify any language features that the author has used. Take feedback, annotate the text (see Resource Page I) and create a class checklist of the features identified (see checklist 3, Resource Page V for ideas).

- Use careful questioning to help identify this feature: **What happens after someone has spoken?**

- Many features in the climax of the story will have already been identified in the opening and build-up.

Independent, pair or guided work

- In pairs, the children find examples of identified checklist features in the second half of chapter 3 and annotate their own text.

Plenary

- Ask the children if they found anything to add to the class checklist. Note: the second part of chapter 3 uses time connectives to move the story on and a question for the reader in addition to the features already identified.

- Select children to give examples of the word and language features they have identified from the checklist.

Writing a Climax

Objective

We will write the climax for our own adventure story

You need: Resource Pages O and Q; OHTs.

Whole class work

- Ask the children to recall five features from the class checklist for writing the climax of the story. Take feedback and display the checklist.

- Remind the children of the notes made for the climax of the adventure story on the story hill (Resource Page Q).

- Reread the opening and build-up of your modelled story (Resource Page O) and discuss whether the climax needs to be changed at all. Make any necessary changes in note form to the story hill.

- Using the story hill planning and the checklist, model writing the climax of your adventure story (Resource Page O). During the modelled writing ensure you:
  - refer to the checklist and ask the children to put their hands up when you have used something on the checklist
  - orally rehearse sentences before putting them to paper
  - make occasional deliberate mistakes, for example, in spelling and punctuation, to highlight and correct any misconceptions
  - explain orally any decisions you make as a writer, for example, the choice of one adjective over another
  - refer to the planning notes
  - involve the children in giving suggestions, such as examples of powerful verbs.

Independent, pair or guided work

- Before working independently the children need to refer to their own story hill, reread their story so far and check if they need to change anything on their notes for the climax.

- Working with their response partners or individually, and using the modelled writing, the class checklist and their planning notes, the children write the climax of their own story.

- Select one or two children to write on OHT.

Plenary

- Use the writing on the OHT to check for features against the checklist and ask the children to check their own work against the checklist.

- Use the writing on the OHT to demonstrate editing and improving writing.

- Give the children a few minutes to go back over their writing and make improvements.

(Pupil copymaster)

House Haunting – chapter 1

"Don't you two go anywhere near that house, it's dangerous!" called Ben's mum as she struggled through the front door, her arms loaded with bags of shopping.

"No, we won't. We're only going to the park," yelled Ben as he and his best friend, Jack, slammed the front door and strolled down the pavement grinning at each other. As soon as they were at the end of the street, they burst out laughing.

"I think we fooled her," sniggered Ben and he quickly glanced around to check no-one was in sight. Breaking into a jog, the two boys hurried down Oak Lane, passing the rusty school gates, the corner shop and you've guessed it … the entrance for the park.

Soon they had reached their destination. A blanket of ivy clung to the crumbling red-brick wall which surrounded the house and the huge iron gates crawled with fierce brambles and tangled briars.

"You open it then, you're the oldest," whispered Jack, nudging Ben towards the gate.

"You're such a wimp," muttered Ben and the gates creaked open as he leant on them. Ben crunched up the gravel drive and passed the wild, weed-infested garden, towards the front door with Jack trudging reluctantly behind him. To his amazement, when he turned the brass door handle, the weathered, wooden door swung open with hardly a squeak.

(Pupil copymaster)

House Haunting – chapter 2

Cautiously, they crept across the creaking floorboards peering into one empty room after another. A musty smell, like brown books in the attic, hung in the air and the damp seemed to cling to their clothes and skin. Small chinks of autumn sunshine beamed through boarded up windows and illuminated enormous spiders' webs that draped themselves, like curtains, from one corner of the ceiling to another.

Ben's voice broke the silence. "Come on, let's investigate upstairs," he whispered excitedly and they tiptoed, one behind the other, up the groaning staircase.

Suddenly, they heard it. They both stopped.

"What was…" Jack's whispered question was interrupted by the sound again. This time it was louder and nearer. Jack grabbed Ben's jumper and tried to pull him back down the stairs.

(Pupil copymaster)

House Haunting – chapter 3

At that moment, Jack screamed and Ben jumped as a mouse scurried across the landing and disappeared under a door. "Just a mouse," Ben informed Jack confidently and he continued up the stairs. Jack's legs wobbled like jelly as he followed.

Upstairs appeared to be much like downstairs, but the light was fading and making it difficult to see.

"I think it's time to go," Jack suggested, making his way to the stairs.

"Not yet," insisted Ben. "There's that room over there." He pointed towards a closed door.

Jack shivered as they turned the handle and the door creaked open. They stepped inside and glanced around. At first, it appeared to be just like the other rooms – empty. But as their eyes adjusted to the gloom, they noticed a large wooden wardrobe on the far wall. Grabbing Jack's arm, Ben strolled across the room towards it. The wardrobe door opened easily and lying in the bottom was … a bundle of carrier bags. Feeling brave, Jack picked one up and shook it. It sounded like thunder in the silence. "Look, nothing. So can we go now?" he pleaded.

"Nothing, you say," laughed Ben and he bent down and retrieved a handful of notes. "Look at all this," he exclaimed. "We'll be rich." He reached into the wardrobe, pulled out the other carrier bags and shook the contents on to the floor. The boys laughed as hundreds of ten pound notes floated around them like confetti.

Suddenly, the door banged shut. The boys were silent. Still. Ben stood up, strode over to the door and turned the handle. It was stuck. He tried again. It did not move.

Jack began to cry. "Crying's not going to help. Come and help me," demanded Ben. But the door was stuck fast.

(Pupil copymaster)

House Haunting – chapter 3 (continued)

For a moment the two boys sat surrounded by the money with only the occasional whimper by Jack breaking the silence. "We might as well pick all this up and put it in the bags," said Ben glumly and grabbing a handful he stuffed the notes back into one of the carrier bags. Jack joined in. "Why are these notes red?" asked Jack, holding them up to the fading light at the window. There was no answer for a moment. "I think it means the money is stolen," replied Ben slowly.

"I wonder who stole it?" pondered Jack, continuing to stuff the red notes into the bags.

"I don't know," replied Ben thoughtfully. "But I hope they don't come looking for it tonight." The boys looked at each other. A shiver crept down Ben's spine. "We need to get out of here quickly," he muttered.

"Help, help!" yelled Ben and Jack together. They pummelled on the door until their hands ached and their voices were hoarse, but no-one came. They tried the door again, heaving with all their might, but it didn't move an inch. Dusk was turning into dark and their only light was the orange glimmer from a streetlight. Soon the boys grew tired. They huddled together by the wardrobe and fell into a doze.

After what seemed like hours, Ben woke with a start. He shook Jack to wake him. There it was. That was what had woken him. The noise. It was different this time. Footsteps, definitely footsteps. Downstairs, floorboards creaked. Someone or something was in the house. The boys gripped each other, frozen with fear. The footsteps got louder, nearer. Ben could hear his heart thumping. Who or what was it? Maybe it was the thieves come to take the money, maybe a black-bearded pirate who had hidden his treasure under the floorboards. Jack whimpered. Neither moved a muscle. They held each other even tighter and sunk against the wardrobe, hoping the darkness would swallow them up.

House Haunting – chapter 4

"Ben! Jack! Are you in here?" came a familiar voice. At first they were too terrified to answer. When the voice came again, Ben answered, but his voice was a weak croak.

"It's my mum," whispered Jack, the relief washing over his face.

"Yes, we're here!" Jack hollered at the top of his voice, standing up and stumbling towards the door. "The door is stuck and there's lots of money in carrier bags and we think it's stolen," Jack rambled, trying to explain the whole situation.

"Stand away from the door," commanded a man's voice. Someone shoved the door from the outside and it flung open to reveal a policeman shining a torch in the direction of the boys. Jack's mum ran towards the boys and hugged them so tightly they were gasping for air when she finally released her grip.

"I think we'll have this," said the policeman, shining his beam on to the plastic bags of money. The policeman closed the door behind them and they all trundled down the stairs and out of the front door, the iron gates clanging shut behind them.

Classworks Literacy Year 3 © Carolyn Bray, Nelson Thornes Ltd 2003

House Haunting – chapter 5

The two boys sat silently in the back of the police car as it drove down the dark, empty streets. Jack's mum said nothing. Ben's mum was at the front door when the police car dropped them off.

"Well, young man, you've got a lot of explaining to do," she snapped, as Ben approached the front door. "I told you not to go near that house." She slammed the front door shut. Ben hung his head.

"I'm sorry, Mum," he mumbled and then looked up and smiled pleadingly. "Can I have a bacon sandwich? I'm really hungry."

(Exemplar analysis)

Example of analysis of *House Haunting – chapter 1*

Story beginning — introduce characters.

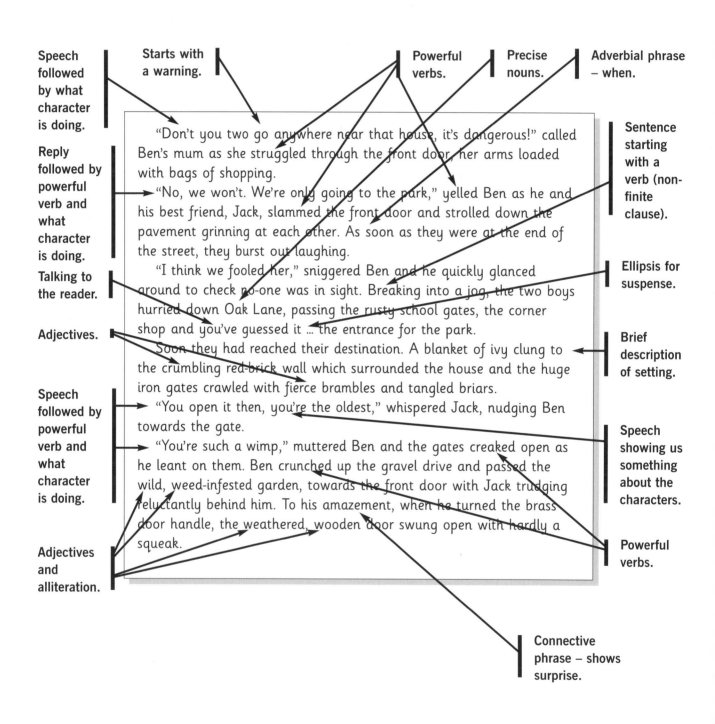

Speech followed by what character is doing.

Starts with a warning.

Powerful verbs.

Precise nouns.

Adverbial phrase – when.

Reply followed by powerful verb and what character is doing.

Talking to the reader.

Adjectives.

Speech followed by powerful verb and what character is doing.

Adjectives and alliteration.

Sentence starting with a verb (non-finite clause).

Ellipsis for suspense.

Brief description of setting.

Speech showing us something about the characters.

Powerful verbs.

Connective phrase – shows surprise.

"Don't you two go anywhere near that house, it's dangerous!" called Ben's mum as she struggled through the front door, her arms loaded with bags of shopping.

"No, we won't. We're only going to the park," yelled Ben as he and his best friend, Jack, slammed the front door and strolled down the pavement grinning at each other. As soon as they were at the end of the street, they burst out laughing.

"I think we fooled her," sniggered Ben and he quickly glanced around to check no-one was in sight. Breaking into a jog, the two boys hurried down Oak Lane, passing the rusty school gates, the corner shop and you've guessed it ... the entrance for the park.

Soon they had reached their destination. A blanket of ivy clung to the crumbling red-brick wall which surrounded the house and the huge iron gates crawled with fierce brambles and tangled briars.

"You open it then, you're the oldest," whispered Jack, nudging Ben towards the gate.

"You're such a wimp," muttered Ben and the gates creaked open as he leant on them. Ben crunched up the gravel drive and passed the wild, weed-infested garden, towards the front door with Jack trudging reluctantly behind him. To his amazement, when he turned the brass door handle, the weathered, wooden door swung open with hardly a squeak.

(Exemplar analysis)

Example of analysis of *House Haunting – chapter 2*

Build-up — describe the setting. End with suspense so the reader wants to read on.

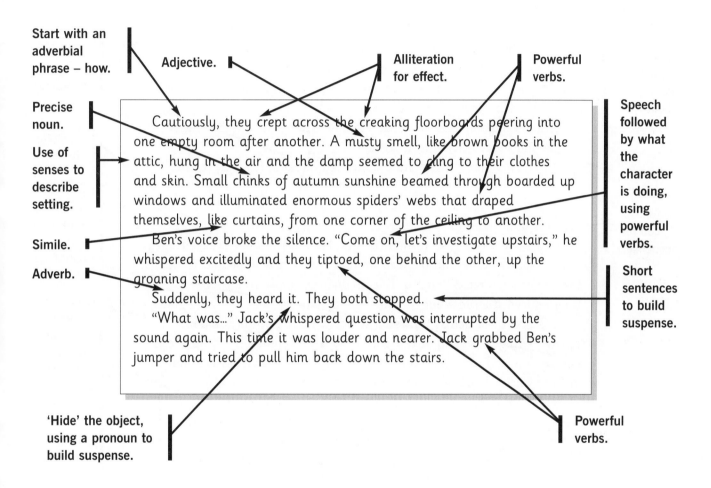

Start with an adverbial phrase – how.

Adjective.

Alliteration for effect.

Powerful verbs.

Precise noun.

Use of senses to describe setting.

Simile.

Adverb.

Speech followed by what the character is doing, using powerful verbs.

Short sentences to build suspense.

Cautiously, they crept across the creaking floorboards peering into one empty room after another. A musty smell, like brown books in the attic, hung in the air and the damp seemed to cling to their clothes and skin. Small chinks of autumn sunshine beamed through boarded up windows and illuminated enormous spiders' webs that draped themselves, like curtains, from one corner of the ceiling to another.

Ben's voice broke the silence. "Come on, let's investigate upstairs," he whispered excitedly and they tiptoed, one behind the other, up the groaning staircase.

Suddenly, they heard it. They both stopped.

"What was..." Jack's whispered question was interrupted by the sound again. This time it was louder and nearer. Jack grabbed Ben's jumper and tried to pull him back down the stairs.

'Hide' the object, using a pronoun to build suspense.

Powerful verbs.

Classworks Literacy Year 3 © Carolyn Bray, Nelson Thornes Ltd 2003

(Exemplar analysis)

Example of analysis of *House Haunting – chapter 3*

Problem or dilemma leading to the climax.

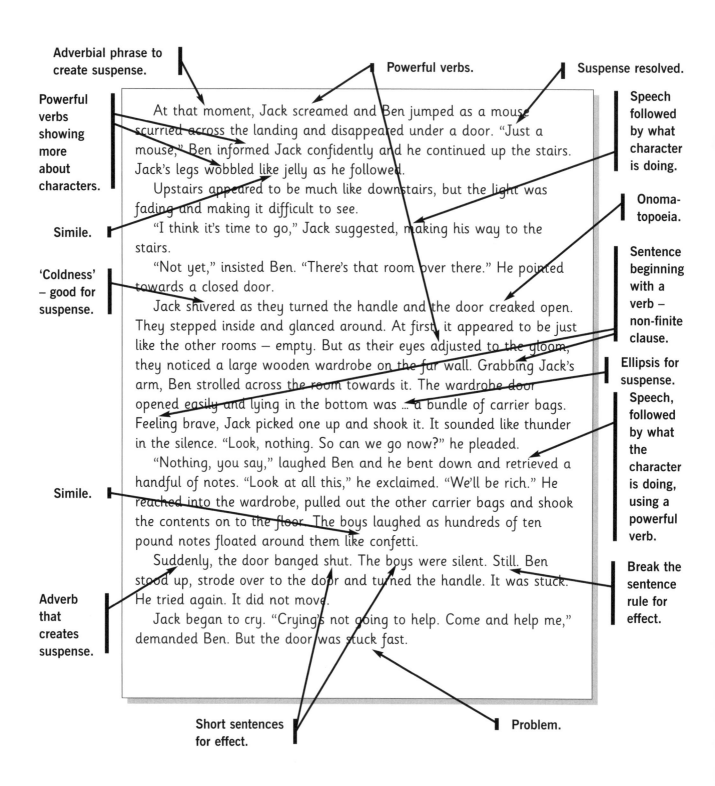

Adverbial phrase to create suspense.

Powerful verbs.

Suspense resolved.

Powerful verbs showing more about characters.

Simile.

'Coldness' – good for suspense.

Simile.

Adverb that creates suspense.

Speech followed by what character is doing.

Onoma-topoeia.

Sentence beginning with a verb – non-finite clause.

Ellipsis for suspense.

Speech, followed by what the character is doing, using a powerful verb.

Break the sentence rule for effect.

At that moment, Jack screamed and Ben jumped as a mouse scurried across the landing and disappeared under a door. "Just a mouse," Ben informed Jack confidently and he continued up the stairs. Jack's legs wobbled like jelly as he followed.

Upstairs appeared to be much like downstairs, but the light was fading and making it difficult to see.

"I think it's time to go," Jack suggested, making his way to the stairs.

"Not yet," insisted Ben. "There's that room over there." He pointed towards a closed door.

Jack shivered as they turned the handle and the door creaked open. They stepped inside and glanced around. At first, it appeared to be just like the other rooms – empty. But as their eyes adjusted to the gloom, they noticed a large wooden wardrobe on the far wall. Grabbing Jack's arm, Ben strolled across the room towards it. The wardrobe door opened easily and lying in the bottom was … a bundle of carrier bags. Feeling brave, Jack picked one up and shook it. It sounded like thunder in the silence. "Look, nothing. So can we go now?" he pleaded.

"Nothing, you say," laughed Ben and he bent down and retrieved a handful of notes. "Look at all this," he exclaimed. "We'll be rich." He reached into the wardrobe, pulled out the other carrier bags and shook the contents on to the floor. The boys laughed as hundreds of ten pound notes floated around them like confetti.

Suddenly, the door banged shut. The boys were silent. Still. Ben stood up, strode over to the door and turned the handle. It was stuck. He tried again. It did not move.

Jack began to cry. "Crying's not going to help. Come and help me," demanded Ben. But the door was stuck fast.

Short sentences for effect.

Problem.

Exemplar analysis

Example of analysis of *House Haunting – chapter 3* (continued)

Building tension.

Adjective.

Connective to move story on.

Powerful verbs.

For a moment the two boys sat surrounded by the money with only the occasional whimper by Jack breaking the silence. "We might as well pick all this up and put it in the bags," said Ben glumly and grabbing a handful he stuffed the notes back into one of the carrier bags. Jack joined in. "Why are these notes red?" asked Jack, holding them up to the fading light at the window. There was no answer for a moment. "I think it means the money is stolen," replied Ben slowly.

"I wonder who stole it?" pondered Jack, continuing to stuff the red notes into the bags.

"I don't know," replied Ben thoughtfully. "But I hope they don't come looking for it tonight." The boys looked at each other. A shiver crept down Ben's spine. "We need to get out of here quickly," he muttered.

"Help, help!" yelled Ben and Jack together. They pummelled on the door until their hands ached and their voices were hoarse, but no-one came. They tried the door again, heaving with all their might, but it didn't move an inch. Dusk was turning into dark and their only light was the orange glimmer from a streetlight. Soon the boys grew tired. They huddled together by the wardrobe and fell into a doze.

After what seemed like hours, Ben woke with a start. He shook Jack to wake him. There it was. That was what had woken him. The noise. It was different this time. Footsteps, definitely footsteps. Downstairs, floorboards creaked. Someone or something was in the house. The boys gripped each other, frozen with fear. The footsteps got louder, nearer. Ben could hear his heart thumping. Who or what was it? Maybe it was the thieves come to take the money, maybe a black-bearded pirate who had hidden his treasure under the floorboards. Jack whimpered. Neither moved a muscle. They held each other even tighter and sunk against the wardrobe, hoping the darkness would swallow them up.

Long sentence after all the short ones.

Coldness/ darkness to create tension.

Short sentences to build suspense.

'Empty' words to create suspense.

Question to draw in the reader.

Adjective.

(Exemplar analysis)

Example of analysis of *House Haunting – chapter 4*

Resolution – help comes unexpectedly.

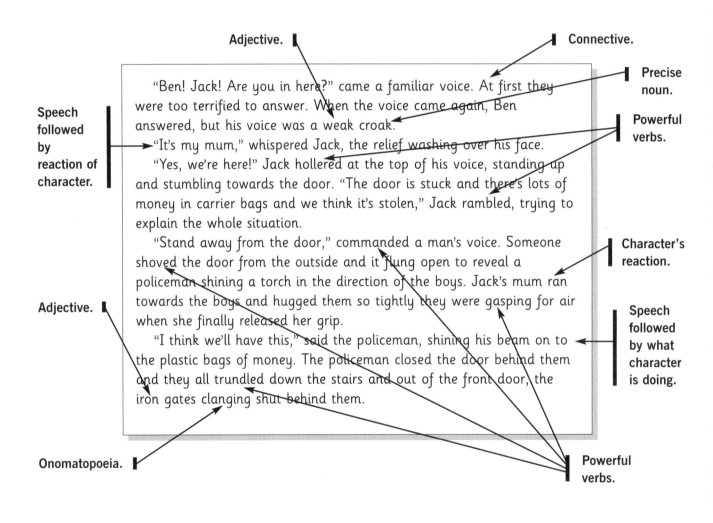

Adjective.

Connective.

Precise noun.

Speech followed by reaction of character.

Powerful verbs.

"Ben! Jack! Are you in here?" came a familiar voice. At first they were too terrified to answer. When the voice came again, Ben answered, but his voice was a weak croak.

"It's my mum," whispered Jack, the relief washing over his face.

"Yes, we're here!" Jack hollered at the top of his voice, standing up and stumbling towards the door. "The door is stuck and there's lots of money in carrier bags and we think it's stolen," Jack rambled, trying to explain the whole situation.

"Stand away from the door," commanded a man's voice. Someone shoved the door from the outside and it flung open to reveal a policeman shining a torch in the direction of the boys. Jack's mum ran towards the boys and hugged them so tightly they were gasping for air when she finally released her grip.

"I think we'll have this," said the policeman, shining his beam on to the plastic bags of money. The policeman closed the door behind them and they all trundled down the stairs and out of the front door, the iron gates clanging shut behind them.

Character's reaction.

Speech followed by what character is doing.

Adjective.

Onomatopoeia.

Powerful verbs.

Classworks Literacy Year 3 © Carolyn Bray, Nelson Thornes Ltd 2003

(Exemplar analysis)

Example of analysis of *House Haunting – chapter 5*

Ending – the characters go home.

Adjectives.

Comment on warning given at beginning of story.

Speech followed by what character does.

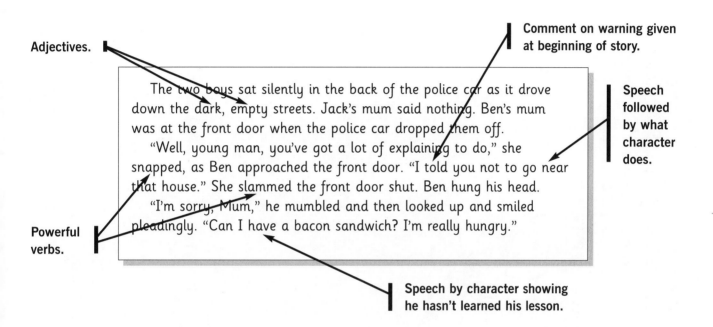

The two boys sat silently in the back of the police car as it drove down the dark, empty streets. Jack's mum said nothing. Ben's mum was at the front door when the police car dropped them off.

"Well, young man, you've got a lot of explaining to do," she snapped, as Ben approached the front door. "I told you not to go near that house." She slammed the front door shut. Ben hung his head.

"I'm sorry, Mum," he mumbled and then looked up and smiled pleadingly. "Can I have a bacon sandwich? I'm really hungry."

Powerful verbs.

Speech by character showing he hasn't learned his lesson.

Classworks Literacy Year 3 © Carolyn Bray, Nelson Thornes Ltd 2003

(**Pupil copymaster**)

Story hill for *House Haunting*

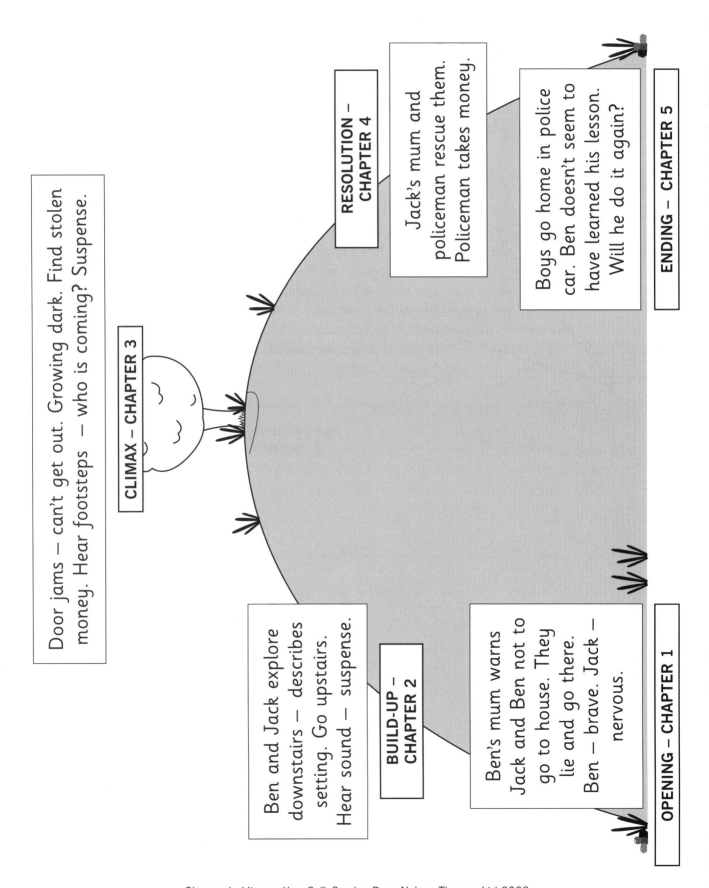

Door jams – can't get out. Growing dark. Find stolen money. Hear footsteps – who is coming? Suspense.

CLIMAX – CHAPTER 3

RESOLUTION – CHAPTER 4

Jack's mum and policeman rescue them. Policeman takes money.

Boys go home in police car. Ben doesn't seem to have learned his lesson. Will he do it again?

ENDING – CHAPTER 5

Ben and Jack explore downstairs – describes setting. Go upstairs. Hear sound – suspense.

BUILD-UP – CHAPTER 2

Ben's mum warns Jack and Ben not to go to house. They lie and go there. Ben – brave. Jack – nervous.

OPENING – CHAPTER 1

(Pupil copymaster)

Story hill

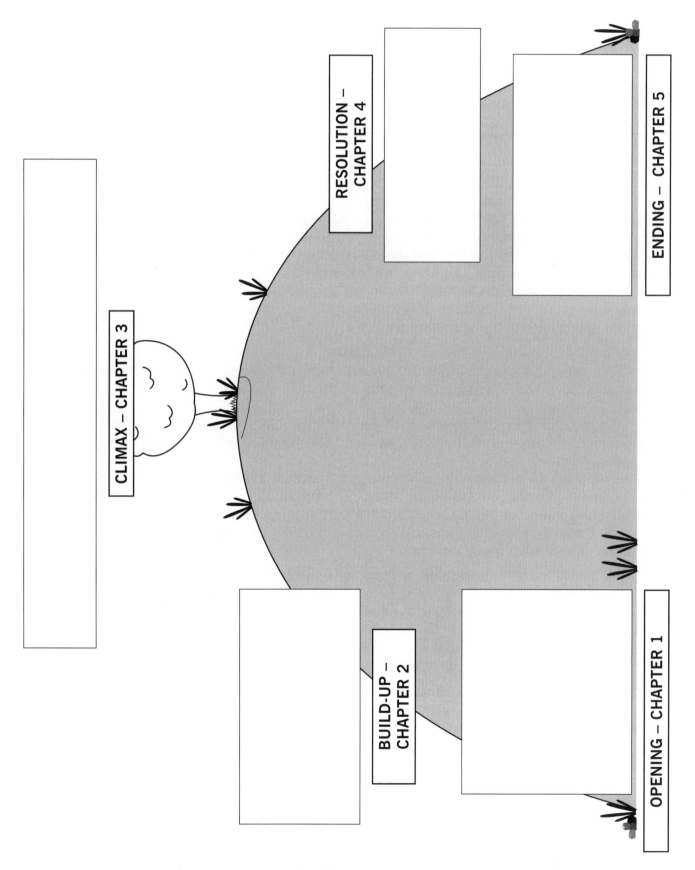

RESOLUTION – CHAPTER 4

ENDING – CHAPTER 5

CLIMAX – CHAPTER 3

BUILD-UP – CHAPTER 2

OPENING – CHAPTER 1

(Exemplar material)

Modelled writing

Opening (Introduce characters)

"Don't go too far you two, you'll get lost," warned Mrs Bailey as she hammered the tent pegs into the ground.

"No, we just want to explore over there," called Becky, pointing to the woods at the edge of the campsite. She grabbed Joe's hand and they dashed off, leaving Mrs Bailey to empty the car and feed Zimber, their labrador.

"I don't want to go in there, it looks scary," whispered Joe nervously as he peered over the fence that surrounded the wood.

"Come on, it's fun to explore," Becky urged and she clambered over the fence with Joe following.

Build-up (Describe setting and end with suspense)

Slowly, they stepped into the still, soundless wood. Above them giant trees towered like city skyscrapers and beneath them their feet slipped and squelched on the muddy pathway. Whispers of wind gently rustled leaves and the fresh scent of recent rainfall filled the air. Step by step, they ventured deeper into the trees, Joe firmly clutching Becky's hand.

Suddenly, the silence was broken. The snap of a twig echoed like thunder around the wood. Becky stood frozen to the spot. Something moved in the undergrowth. It was coming nearer. Joe hid his face against her arm, too scared to look.

Climax

At that moment, a grey squirrel darted in front of them and scurried up a nearby tree. Becky breathed a sigh of relief. Peeking out from under Becky's arm, Joe whispered, "I want to go back now."

"Let's go just a little bit further. You never know, we might see a badger or a deer. Wouldn't that be exciting?" persuaded Becky. "Come on, let's run." She raced deeper into the wood with Joe following reluctantly.

After a while, the sun began to sink in the sky. It grew dark and difficult to see. All of a sudden, Becky tripped and stumbled. She tried to stand, but cried out with pain and collapsed on to a pile of damp, rotting leaves. Joe began to cry. Then they both heard it. The snap of twigs. The crackle of bracken. Someone or something was coming in their direction. They sat perfectly still, hardly daring to breath. Who or what was it?

Resolution (Help comes unexpectedly)

The next thing they felt was the warm, wet tongue of a dog slobbering over their faces. "Zimber, it's you!" spluttered Joe, still snivelling. Becky and Joe stroked and hugged him. A few seconds later, the beam of a torch blinded them. "So he found you then," said Mum, trying to hide her relief. She decided that Becky had only twisted her ankle and gave her a piggy-back ride through the dark, moonlit wood, back to the campsite. Zimber led the way with Joe and the torch.

Ending (Characters go home)

"That's the last time you two go off exploring on this holiday, said Mrs Bailey angrily, as she bandaged Becky's swollen ankle back in their tent. "It's a good job Zimber found you, otherwise you would have been there all night." Joe began to cry again. "I don't like exploring," he snivelled and hugged his mum.

"Well, I do like exploring, it's exciting," insisted Becky, limping to her sleeping bag. As she snuggled down, she was already planning where to explore in the morning, but this time she thought that she would take Zimber.

Classworks Literacy Year 3 © Carolyn Bray, Nelson Thornes Ltd 2003

(Exemplar material)

Example of analysis of modelled writing

Speech followed by what the character is doing.

Reply by character followed by what she is doing.

Start with an adverb: 'how'.

Alliteration for effect.

Adverb that creates suspense.

Onomatopoeia.

Adverbial phrase for suspense.

Time connective to move story on.

Adjectives.

Question for the reader.

Help comes unexpectedly.

Speech followed by what character is doing.

Commenting on the warning given at the beginning.

Characters go 'home'.

Starts with a warning.   **Introduce characters.**   **Powerful verbs.**   **Hints at setting.**

Speech showing something about the character, followed by what he is doing.

What reader 'sees'.

Adverbial phrase: 'how'

Short sentence and 'empty' words to create suspense.

Suspense resolved.

Sentence starting with a verb (non finite clause).

Darkness to build tension.

Time connective to move story on.

Character's reaction.

Adjectives.

Comment on the resolution.

Character has learned his lesson.

Character has learned her lesson.

Speech showing characteristics haven't changed.   **Powerful verbs.**

Opening

"Don't go too far you two, you'll get lost," warned Mrs Bailey as she hammered the tent pegs into the ground.

"No, we just want to explore over there," called Becky, pointing to the woods at the edge of the campsite. She grabbed Joe's hand and they dashed off, leaving Mrs Bailey to empty the car and feed Zimber, their labrador.

"I don't want to go in there, it looks scary," whispered Joe nervously as he peered over the fence that surrounded the wood.

"Come on, it's fun to explore," Becky urged and she clambered over the fence with Joe following.

Build-up

Slowly, they stepped into the still, soundless wood. Above them giant trees towered like city skyscrapers and beneath them their feet slipped and squelched on the muddy pathway. Whispers of wind gently rustled leaves and the fresh scent of recent rainfall filled the air. Step by step, they ventured deeper into the trees, Joe firmly clutching Becky's hand.

Suddenly, the silence was broken. The snap of a twig echoed like thunder around the wood. Becky stood frozen to the spot. Something moved in the undergrowth. It was coming nearer. Joe hid his face against her arm, too scared to look.

Climax

At that moment, a grey squirrel darted in front of them and scurried up a nearby tree. Becky breathed a sigh of relief. Peeking out from under Becky's arm, Joe whispered, "I want to go back now."

"Let's go just a little bit further. You never know, we might see a badger or a deer. Wouldn't that be exciting?" persuaded Becky. "Come on, let's run." She raced deeper into the wood with Joe following reluctantly.

After a while, the sun began to sink in the sky. It grew dark and difficult to see. All of a sudden, Becky tripped and stumbled. She tried to stand, but cried out with pain and collapsed on to a pile of damp, rotting leaves. Joe began to cry. Then they both heard it. The snap of twigs. The crackle of bracken. Someone or something was coming in their direction. They sat perfectly still, hardly daring to breath. Who or what was it?

Resolution

The next thing they felt was the warm, wet tongue of a dog slobbering over their faces. "Zimber, it's you!" spluttered Joe, still snivelling. Becky and Joe stroked and hugged him. A few seconds later, the beam of a torch blinded them. "So he found you then," said Mum, trying to hide her relief. She decided that Becky had only twisted her ankle and gave her a piggy-back ride through the dark, moonlit wood, back to the campsite. Zimber led the way with Joe and the torch.

Ending

"That's the last time you two go off exploring on this holiday," said Mrs Bailey angrily, as she bandaged Becky's swollen ankle back in their tent. "It's a good job Zimber found you, otherwise you would have been there all night." Joe began to cry again. "I don't like exploring," he snivelled and hugged his mum.

"Well, I do like exploring, it's exciting," insisted Becky, limping to her sleeping bag. As she snuggled down, she was already planning where to explore in the morning, but this time she thought that she would take Zimber.

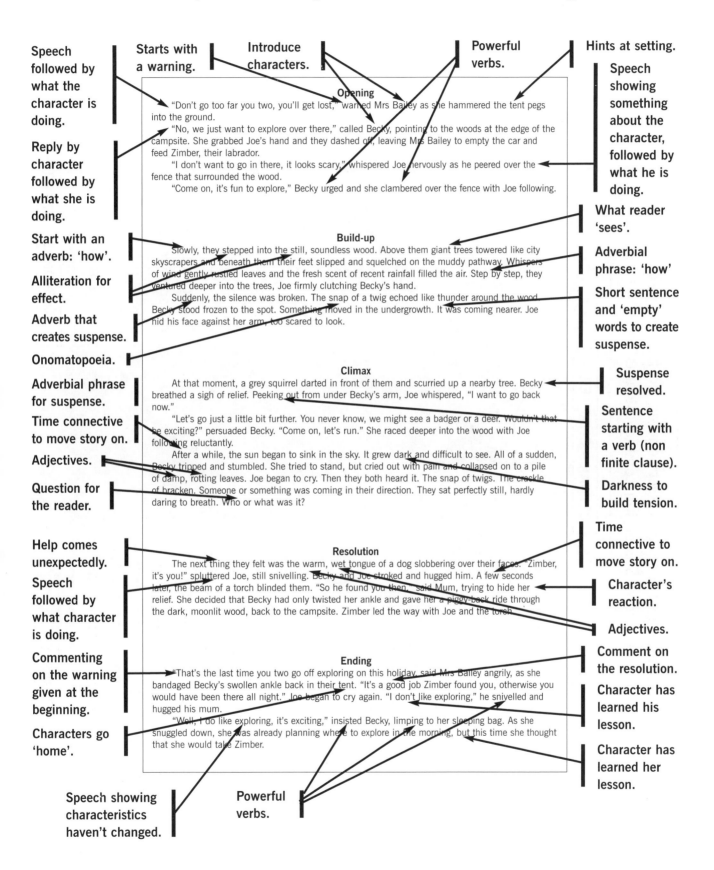

(Exemplar material)

Story hill for modelled writing

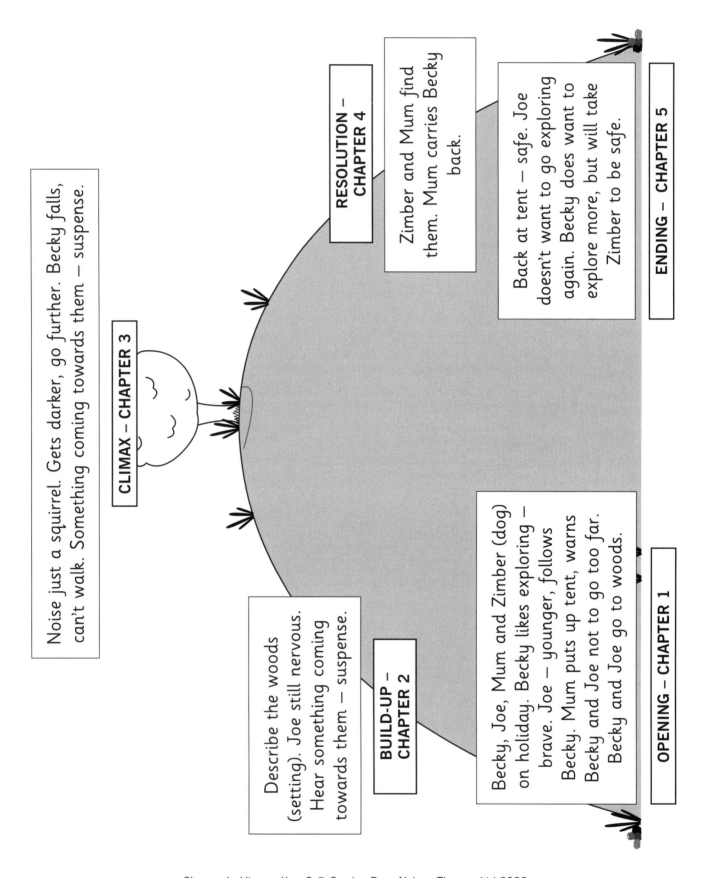

CLIMAX – CHAPTER 3

Noise just a squirrel. Gets darker, go further. Becky falls, can't walk. Something coming towards them – suspense.

RESOLUTION – CHAPTER 4

Zimber and Mum find them. Mum carries Becky back.

ENDING – CHAPTER 5

Back at tent – safe. Joe doesn't want to go exploring again. Becky does want to explore more, but will take Zimber to be safe.

BUILD-UP – CHAPTER 2

Describe the woods (setting). Joe still nervous. Hear something coming towards them – suspense.

OPENING – CHAPTER 1

Becky, Joe, Mum and Zimber (dog) on holiday. Becky likes exploring – brave. Joe – younger, follows Becky. Mum puts up tent, warns Becky and Joe not to go too far. Becky and Joe go to woods.

(Pupil copymaster)

Extracts

1 Very, very slowly, he walked forward into the great forest. Giant trees were soon surrounding him on all sides and their branches made an almost solid roof high above his head, blotting out the sky. Here and there little shafts of sunlight shone through gaps in the roof. There was not a sound anywhere. It was like being among dead men in an enormous empty green cathedral.

When he had ventured some distance into the forest, Little Billy stopped and stood quite still, listening. He could hear nothing. Nothing at all. There was absolute silence. Or was there?

Hold on just one second.

What was that?

Little Billy flicked his head round and stared into the everlasting gloom and doom of the forest. There it was again! There was no mistaking it this time.

from Minpins, *by Roald Dahl*

2 Dimanche Diller woke up suddenly. Moonlight streamed in through her open window. Her bedroom was tucked under the eaves of Hilton Hall, directly below the attic, and she could feel the silence of the empty rooms all round her. She got up, leaned her elbows on the window sill, and pushed her curly dark hair out of her eyes. Everything was still and quiet. Everything felt perfectly normal … or as normal as things do, by night.

Somewhere in Monks Wood a dog barked. Down in the village a door banged. The milk train clanked towards Rockford Market. These were the familiar night noises of the Hilton Valley and they had not woken Dimanche. No. Something quieter, something nearer, had crept into her mind and whispered danger.

from Dimanche Diller, *by Henrietta Branford*

(Exemplar analysis)

Example of analysis of three extracts

All three extracts are examples of story build-up.

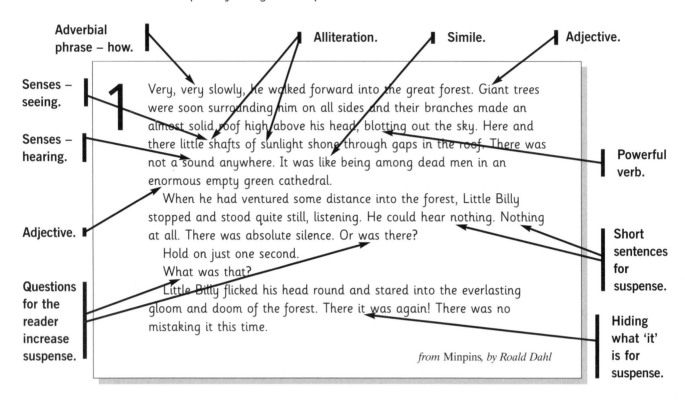

Adverbial phrase – how.

Alliteration.

Simile.

Adjective.

Senses – seeing.

Senses – hearing.

Adjective.

Questions for the reader increase suspense.

Powerful verb.

Short sentences for suspense.

Hiding what 'it' is for suspense.

1 Very, very slowly, he walked forward into the great forest. Giant trees were soon surrounding him on all sides and their branches made an almost solid roof high above his head, blotting out the sky. Here and there little shafts of sunlight shone through gaps in the roof. There was not a sound anywhere. It was like being among dead men in an enormous empty green cathedral.
When he had ventured some distance into the forest, Little Billy stopped and stood quite still, listening. He could hear nothing. Nothing at all. There was absolute silence. Or was there?
    Hold on just one second.
    What was that?
Little Billy flicked his head round and stared into the everlasting gloom and doom of the forest. There it was again! There was no mistaking it this time.

from Minpins, *by Roald Dahl*

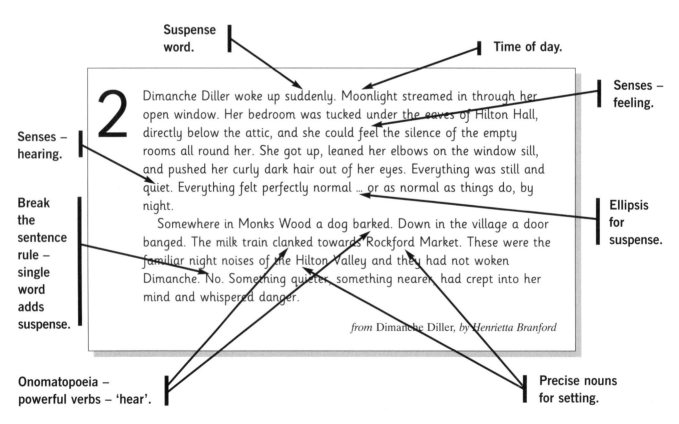

Suspense word.

Time of day.

Senses – feeling.

Senses – hearing.

Break the sentence rule – single word adds suspense.

Ellipsis for suspense.

2 Dimanche Diller woke up suddenly. Moonlight streamed in through her open window. Her bedroom was tucked under the eaves of Hilton Hall, directly below the attic, and she could feel the silence of the empty rooms all round her. She got up, leaned her elbows on the window sill, and pushed her curly dark hair out of her eyes. Everything was still and quiet. Everything felt perfectly normal ... or as normal as things do, by night.
    Somewhere in Monks Wood a dog barked. Down in the village a door banged. The milk train clanked towards Rockford Market. These were the familiar night noises of the Hilton Valley and they had not woken Dimanche. No. Something quieter, something nearer, had crept into her mind and whispered danger.

from Dimanche Diller, *by Henrietta Branford*

Onomatopoeia – powerful verbs – 'hear'.

Precise nouns for setting.

(Pupil copymaster)

Chips and Jessie

"Shh! What's that?" interrupted Chips. They both sat, silent. Over by the sink came a noise exactly like the one Jessie was describing – scratch, scratch, scratch!

Then the noise stopped. Nothing happened. Jessie started to go on with her story. The noise started again, louder.

"It's coming from just there, by the taps," said Chips.

They went over to look. Silence. They waited in the gathering dark. Before long they heard it – scratch, scratch, scratch!

Jessie was holding on to Chips very tightly. Something or somebody was coming through the wall!

Shirley Hughes

(Exemplar analysis)

Example of analysis of *Chips and Jessie*

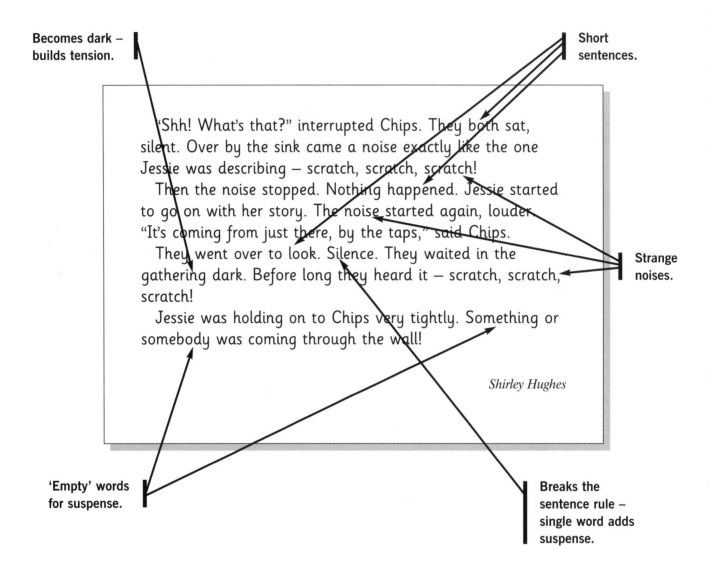

**Becomes dark –
builds tension.**

**Short
sentences.**

'Shh! What's that?" interrupted Chips. They both sat, silent. Over by the sink came a noise exactly like the one Jessie was describing – scratch, scratch, scratch!

Then the noise stopped. Nothing happened. Jessie started to go on with her story. The noise started again, louder. "It's coming from just there, by the taps," said Chips.

They went over to look. Silence. They waited in the gathering dark. Before long they heard it – scratch, scratch, scratch!

Jessie was holding on to Chips very tightly. Something or somebody was coming through the wall!

Shirley Hughes

**Strange
noises.**

**'Empty' words
for suspense.**

**Breaks the
sentence rule –
single word adds
suspense.**

(Exemplar material)

Checklists for adventure stories

Example of a checklist for an adventure story opening ①

- Start with a warning

- Introduce the characters

- Use speech to show something about the characters

- Follow speech by showing what the character is doing

- Use powerful verbs

- Give a hint of the setting

Example of a checklist for a story build-up ②

- Move characters to where 'the adventure' will take place

- Describe the setting using senses

- Use powerful verbs

- Use alliteration

- Use imagery: simile and metaphor

- Start sentences with adverb/adverbial phrases telling how, when or where

- Use onomatopoeia

- Use adverbial phrases that create suspense – for example, 'suddenly'

- Use short sentences to create suspense

- Use 'empty' words or pronouns to create suspense – for example, 'it', 'something'

Example of a checklist for problem/dilemma/climax ③

- Use time connectives to move story on

- Use powerful verbs

- Resolve suspense from previous chapter

- Use long sentences to slow pace

- Use speech to show the reader about the character

- Follow speech by what the character is doing

- Start a sentence with a verb – non-finite clause

- Create suspense by using short sentences, including one word

- Use adverbs, for example, 'suddenly', to create suspense

- Use 'empty' words to create suspense, for example, 'someone' or 'something'

- Show characters' reactions to events

- Use ellipses for suspense

- Refer to coldness or darkness to build tension

- Use simile, adjectives and onomatopoeia to describe

- Use a question to draw in the reader

Continued ...

(Exemplar material)

Further checklists for adventure stories

Example of a checklist for a story resolution ④

- Have help coming unexpectedly
- Use speech followed by what the character is doing
- Describe character's reaction
- Use powerful verbs
- Use adjectives and onomatopoeia for description
- Use connectives

Example of a checklist for a story ending ⑤

- Have the characters 'go home'
- Use speech or what the character is thinking to show whether they have learnt their lesson
- Have one character referring back to the warning they gave
- Follow speech with what the character does
- Use powerful verbs
- Use adjectives to describe

(**Marking ladder**)

Name: _____

Pupil	Objective	Teacher
	In my adventure story I have written five chapters: opening, build-up, climax, resolution and ending.	
	My ending mentions the warning given at the start.	
	I used suspense at the end of at least one chapter.	
	I used speech and powerful verbs to describe characters.	
	I followed the speech of a character by describing what they are doing using a powerful verb.	
	I started sentences in different ways – for example, with an adverbial phrase (how, when, where), a connective or a verb (non-finite clause).	
	I chose adjectives, simile and precise nouns to describe.	
	I used alliteration and onomatopoeia to give sound effects.	
	I used some short sentences and some long sentences.	
	I used speech marks correctly.	
	I presented my story attractively and included a title page and author details.	
	What could I do to improve my story next time?	

Word-level starter activities

Which one?

- Write down a few words on the board, for example, 'wos', 'was', 'wass', 'waz'. The children write the correct word and show you. *How do you remember the correct spelling?*

Robot

- Talk like a Dalek, reading out different words, segmenting each phoneme clearly. Point to the children in turn and challenge them to spell the word letter by letter.

I Spy

- Play a game of 'I Spy', but use the final sound and/or first sound of a word, rather than how it is spelt.

Phoneme count

- Read out a word and ask the children to count the phonemes as you do so. Alternatively, write words on the board and ask the children to say how many phonemes each has. Then read them out as a class to check.

Rhyme it

- Write a word on the board. The children have 30 seconds to write as many words as they can that rhyme with this word.

Word builders

- Give prefix or suffix and challenge the children to build as many words as they can.

Present to past

- Write a sentence in present tense and ask the children to write in the past tense, for example, 'I run' to 'I ran'. Repeat the other way around if appropriate.

Shannon's game

- Write the first letter of a word on the board and write dashes after that letter, one to represent each letter. Allow the class ten guesses (or adapt as appropriate) for the next letter, based on their knowledge of word formation. If they do not guess correctly, write in the letter for them and go on to the next. Concentrate on different sorts of word, for example, guessing that 'q - - - -' is 'qu - - -'; guessing that 't - - -' could be 'th - -', 'to - -', 'ta - -', 'te - -', 'tu - -', 'tr - -', 'ti - -', 'tw - -', 'ty - -' and so on.

Picture it

- This game can be used to help children with 'difficult' words. Write a word on the board. The children look at it and make a picture in their mind of how the word is written. Seat 'strugglers' so they look up to the left of the board. Question the children to build up strategies for the whole class.

Reveal

- This is a variation of Shannon's game. Write a word on the board and, using a piece of card or a similar screen, reveal a word one letter at a time for the children to guess.

Speed write

- Write a word on the board. Look at it carefully as a class and talk about strategies for learning the word. Give different children 30 seconds to write it on the board as many times as they can.

Word of the day

- Choose a word (cross-curricular) that the children are spelling incorrectly, and discuss strategies that different children use or could use to remember it.

I'm thinking of a word

- This is a variation of 'I'm thinking of a number'. One child chooses a word from a group of words, and the other children ask questions to work out what the word might be. For example, 'How many phonemes?', 'How many letters?', 'Does it have a prefix?', 'Is it an adjective?', 'What's the final sound?'

Word creation

- Use large letters (such as those provided at the back of *Progression in Phonics*, or large foam letters) – one for each child. Call out a word, and the children group together to make that word correctly. This game can be played on the playground.

Rhymes

- Create rhymes for words based on their individual letters. For example, a poem rhyming the word 'difficulty' letter by-letter: 'Mrs D, Mrs I, Mrs F, F, I, Mrs C, Mrs U, Mrs L, T, Y' (from *Matilda*).

Car registrations

- Create words from random sets of consonants, for example, from car registration plates. Letters have to appear in the same order as they do on the number plate, for example, R M B = 'remember'.

Countdown

- Play a letters game similar to that on the TV game show. The children choose a certain number of vowels and consonants from cards at random, set a timer and then, working in pairs or alone, make up as many words as they can from those letters, or see what is the longest word they can make.

Chain letter

- Start with a word, then go round the class, the children creating a new word each time by changing one letter.

Words within words

- Write a selection of words onto a flip chart. Ask the class to identify any smaller words within those words, for example, 'howls' ('owl'), 'barks' ('ark'), 'roars' ('oar') and so on.

Anagrams

- Mix up a word and challenge the children to unscramble it. Then challenge the children to set their own anagrams for the rest of the class.

Sentence-level starter activities

Making sentences

- Put a word on the board, for example, 'dog'. Ask the children to write the beginning of a sentence using this word, for example, 'The dog'. Add another word to the board and ask the children to continue their sentence using this word, then add another, and so on. You can play this on many levels adding a variety of words, for example, 'shark', 'jelly', 'whispered', 'because' and so on.

Boring sentences

- Give the children a dull sentence to improve, for example, 'The man got out of the car.' Encourage them to rewrite the sentence in a different genre, for example, as a headline, an instruction, part of a report and so on.

Sentence doctor

- Choose a phrase or sentence with a common error, for example, 'He could of danced all night.' Ask the children to be a 'sentence doctor' and 'fix' the sentence.

Joining sentences

- Give a selection of connectives to the class. Then give two small sentences and ask the children to join them with one of the connectives. You can limit the connectives they use as appropriate, for example, challenging them to join 'The car stopped.'/'The robber jumped out.', without using 'and' or 'then'.

Imitating sentences

- Write a sentence or part of a sentence on the board, for example, 'Struggling to stay awake, the teachers …' Ask the children to write their own sentence or phrase using this structure, for example, 'Battling to remain calm, the children …'

Marking ladder

Name: _____

Pupil	Objective	Teacher
	What could I do to improve my work next time?	